WORLD OF GRAMMAR AND WRITING

2

Australia • Brazil • Mexico • Singapore • United Kingdom • United States

Contents

Grammar

1	Present simple and present continuous	**page 4**
2	Past simple and *used to*	**page 12**
3	Past continuous and past simple	**page 20**
4	Present perfect simple	**page 26**
	Grammar review 1	**page 32**
5	Past simple and present perfect simple	**page 36**
6	Future tenses	**page 42**
7	*Can*, *could* and *be able to*	**page 48**
8	*Must/mustn't* and *have to/don't have to*	**page 54**
	Grammar review 2	**page 60**
9	Relative clauses	**page 64**
10	Nouns and articles	**page 68**
11	Quantifiers, *too* and *enough*	**page 74**
12	Past perfect simple	**page 80**
	Grammar review 3	**page 88**
13	Questions and *so/neither*	**page 92**
14	*Should/shouldn't* and *may/might*	**page 100**
15	First and second conditionals	**page 104**
16	Prepositions and reflexive pronouns	**page 110**
	Grammar review 4	**page 114**
17	Gerunds and infinitives	**page 118**
18	Passive voice	**page 124**
19	Comparatives, superlatives and adverbs of manner	**page 130**
20	Present perfect continuous	**page 136**
	Grammar review 5	**page 140**

Writing

1	Description: writing about your favourite person	page 144
2	Story: narrative about an event involving free-time activities	page 146
3	Story: describing a day out (seasonal weather, actions and feelings)	page 148
4	Letter: writing to a friend about plans for a shopping trip and a visit	page 150
5	Article: writing about things to do with school	page 152
6	Email: writing about a health problem	page 154
7	Letter of invitation: writing about plans for a party and inviting	page 156
8	Leaflet: writing about an environmental club	page 158
9	Diary entry: writing about a school visit to a workplace	page 160
10	Composition (narrative): writing about a project using clothes to help others	page 162
	Irregular verbs	**page 164**
	Notes	**page 165**

UNIT 1
Present simple and present continuous

Present simple

Affirmative	Negative	Question
I work	I do not (don't) work	Do I work?
you work	you do not (don't) work	Do you work?
he works	he does not (doesn't) work	Does he work?
she works	she does not (doesn't) work	Does she work?
it works	it does not (doesn't) work	Does it work?
we work	we do not (don't) work	Do we work?
you work	you do not (don't) work	Do you work?
they work	they do not (don't) work	Do they work?

Short answers

Yes, I/you do.   No, I/you don't.
Yes, he/she/it does. No, he/she/it doesn't.
Yes, we/you/they do. No, we/you/they don't.

We use the present simple to talk about:

- habits.
  *He often **goes** to the cinema.*
  *I **walk** in the park every day.*

- general truths.
  *Water **boils** at one hundred degrees Celsius.*
  *We **make** oil from olives.*

- permanent situations in the present.
  *They **live** in Shanghai.*
  *She **teaches** history and geography.*

I usually jog three times a week, but today I'm working out at the gym.

Present simple and present continuous — Unit 1

1 Complete the sentences with the present simple.

1. They _____travel_____ (travel) to town by bus.
2. He _____ (go) to Italy for his holidays.
3. It _____ (rain) in winter.
4. My grandmother _____ (live) in a village in the mountains.
5. I _____ (not eat) eggs for breakfast.
6. Plants _____ (die) without water.
7. The waiter _____ (not work) in an office.
8. Sally _____ (study) for three hours every evening.
9. She _____ (not play) the piano.
10. Lee _____ (speak) English and French.

Think about it!

Remember to add -s or -es for *he*, *she* and *it*. Remember to use *does not/doesn't* for negatives with *he*, *she* and *it*. Remember to use *Does* for questions with *he*, *she* and *it*.

2 Complete the questions with *do* or *does*.

1. _____Do_____ they go on holiday in the summer?
2. _____ he draw nice pictures?
3. _____ you usually do the cooking?
4. _____ your best friend live near you?
5. _____ John have music lessons?
6. _____ Layla help you with your work?
7. _____ she send emails to her friend every day?
8. _____ the sun rise in the east?

3 Write questions.

1. Does he live in the city?
   Yes, he lives in the city.
2. _____
   Yes, she gets up early on Mondays.
3. _____
   Yes, they have lunch at one o'clock.
4. _____
   No, Jakub doesn't drive a car.

Unit 1 — Present simple and present continuous

Present continuous

Affirmative	Negative	Question
I am (I'm) working	I am not (I'm not) working	Am I working?
you are (you're) working	you are not (aren't) working	Are you working?
he is (he's) working	he is not (isn't) working	Is he working?
she is (she's) working	she is not (isn't) working	Is she working?
it is (it's) working	it is not (isn't) working	Is it working?
we are (we're) working	we are not (aren't) working	Are we working?
you are (you're) working	you are not (aren't) working	Are you working?
they are (they're) working	they are not (aren't) working	Are they working?

Short answers

Yes, I am.	No, I'm not.
Yes, you are.	No, you aren't.
Yes, he/she/it is.	No, he/she/it isn't.
Yes, we/you/they/are.	No, we/you/they aren't.

We use the present continuous to talk about:

- things happening at the time of speaking.
  She **is watching** a fashion show at the moment.
  I **am not reading** the newspaper; I **am reading** a book.

- things happening in our lives, but not necessarily at the exact time we are speaking.
  We**'re studying** Italian this year.
  She**'s working** in a bank for the summer.

4 Complete the sentences with *am*, *are* or *is*.

1 Adriana ____is____ driving here.
2 _____ you writing a letter?
3 I _____ not working in the hotel this summer.
4 My friends _____ watching a film.
5 He _____ tidying his room.
6 They _____ playing football.
7 We _____ waiting for our friends to arrive.
8 She _____ not listening to the radio.

5 Write questions.

1 You are making a cake for me.
  Are you making a cake for me?
2 They are wearing nice clothes.
  _____
3 He is cooking lunch for the family.
  _____
4 The children are swimming in the sea.
  _____
5 She is watering the flowers.
  _____
6 We are driving to the beach.
  _____

Present simple and present continuous — Unit 1

6 Write the sentences using the short form of the verbs.

1 We are not eating lunch.
   We aren't eating lunch.

2 They are not listening to the teacher.
   _____

3 I am not learning Spanish or Italian.
   _____

4 My brother is not reading a comic.
   _____

5 She is not cleaning her car.
   _____

6 I am not wearing your shirt.
   _____

7 Complete the sentences with the present continuous.

1 The neighbours __are building__ (build) a new house.
2 It is Saturday. We _____ (not work) today.
3 _____ the baby _____ (sleep)?
4 Be quiet! I _____ (listen) to the radio.
5 We _____ (not paint) the bedroom green.
6 I _____ (write) an email to my friends in England.
7 'Where is Jenny?' 'She _____ (wait) for us at the house.'
8 It is Hugo's birthday. He _____ (have) a party.

Unit 1 Present simple and present continuous

Adverbs of frequency with the present simple

never	rarely	sometimes	often	usually	always
0%					100%

Adverbs of frequency come before the main verb but after the verb *to be*.
I **never go** to concerts.
My brother **is often** tired at the end of the day.

8 Rewrite the sentences with the adverbs of frequency in the correct place.

1 He is at home at the weekend. (rarely)
   He is rarely at home at the weekend.

2 I buy my mum flowers for her birthday. (usually)
   _____

3 Juan does his homework on the right day. (never)
   _____

4 I am late for work. (always)
   _____

5 Does she get home late on Fridays? (often)
   _____

6 Mr Morris plays the piano at concerts. (sometimes)
   _____

Time expressions with the present simple

at the weekend	every week	once a week
every day	in June	on Mondays
every month	in the afternoon	three times a day
every summer	in the evening	twice a month
every year	in the morning	

Do you work **at the weekend**?
She doesn't wash the dishes **every day**.

Time expressions with the present continuous

at the moment	this morning
now	this week
right now	this year
this afternoon	today
this month	

I am washing the car **at the moment**.
Akil and Sara are staying with us **this week**.

Present simple and present continuous — Unit 1

9 Complete the table with the words and expressions from the box.

> ~~always~~   ~~at the moment~~   every week   now   often   on Saturdays   rarely
> right now   this evening   this year   today   twice a month

Present simple	Present continuous
always	at the moment

10 Complete the sentences with the present simple or present continuous.

1 The teacher ____is telling____ (tell) the students about the test at the moment.
2 She _____ (travel) to London by train every day.
3 I _____ (do) a project about fashion this week.
4 The film director _____ (not make) an animation at the moment.
5 They _____ (not get up) early at the weekend.
6 _____ you _____ (watch) a film right now?
7 Fiona _____ (come) to the office once a week.
8 Misha rarely _____ (go) on holiday.

Think about it!

Remember to use the correct form of *to be* plus *-ing* for sentences in the present continuous.

Stative verbs

We do not usually use stative verbs with the present continuous. Common stative verbs are:

- verbs of feeling:
  feel, hear, see, smell, sound, taste.
  The soup **smells** wonderful.
  I **see** a lot of children in the park.

- verbs of emotion:
  dislike, hate, like, love, need, prefer, want.
  They **love** swimming in the sea.
  I **prefer** cycling to rowing.

- verbs of understanding:
  appear, believe, forget, hope, imagine, know, mean, remember, seem, think, understand.
  I don't **know** what you mean.
  She doesn't **remember** his name.

- verbs which show possession:
  belong to, own.
  I **own** a red sports car.
  This suitcase **belongs** to my mother.

Unit 1 — Present simple and present continuous

11 Circle the correct answer.

1 This book *belongs* / *is belonging* to me.
2 Jane *writes* / *is writing* an email at the moment.
3 Yes, I *see* / *am seeing* what you mean.
4 She is playing the piano. It *is sounding* / *sounds* nice.
5 *Do you think* / *Are you thinking* this is an interesting book?
6 They *are washing* / *wash* the car today.
7 The children *eat* / *are eating* their lunch now.
8 I *hope* / *am hoping* you are right.

12 Complete the sentences with the present simple or present continuous.

1 _____Do_____ you usually _____ride_____ (ride) your bike to work?
2 _____ you _____ (help) Jane with her work today?
3 Sanaa _____ (not play) the violin very well.
4 We all _____ (go) to a restaurant on Saturday evenings.
5 Look! The cat _____ (chase) the mouse!
6 _____ she _____ (do) the shopping every Friday?
7 They always _____ (go) swimming at the weekend.
8 I _____ (hope) you can come to the party with me.

13 Find the mistakes in the sentences. Then write them correctly.

1 I <u>am</u> usually <u>having</u> dinner at eight o'clock.
  <u>I usually have dinner at eight o'clock.</u>
2 His sister work in a hospital.
  _____
3 Does she likes football?
  _____
4 What do your brother doing at the moment?
  _____
5 I starting work at nine o'clock every morning.
  _____
6 I am knowing him very well.
  _____

Present simple and present continuous — Unit 1

14 Circle the correct answer.

1 I ___ wash my hair every day.
  a right now   (b) usually
2 ___ Mum speaking to her sister on the phone?
  a Is   b Does
3 We ___ shopping on Saturdays.
  a are always going   b always go
4 He is listening to his favourite music ___ .
  a sometimes   b now
5 This is a wonderful party. I ___ a great time!
  a have   b am having
6 My friends ___ social media every day.
  a don't use   b aren't using

15 Write the words in the correct order.

1 clean / I / on / my / always / room / Sundays
  <u>I always clean my room on Sundays.</u>
2 often / we / at / pizza / weekend / eat / the
  _____
3 your / watch TV / does / sister / every day / ?
  _____
4 watching / you / this / are / programme / ?
  _____
5 tired / evenings / is / Friday / she / on / usually
  _____
6 now / right / school / you / going / are / to / ?
  _____

Pairwork

Work in pairs. Tell your partner two things you do every day, two things you sometimes do and two things you never do.

Writing

Complete the sentences in your own words.

1 I often _____.
2 My family never _____.
3 At the moment, my friend _____.
4 On Saturdays, I _____.
5 Every evening, we _____.
6 Our teacher _____.
7 I sometimes _____.
8 In summer, _____.

UNIT 2
Past simple and *used to*

Past simple: regular verbs

Affirmative	Negative	Question
I finished	I did not (didn't) finish	Did I finish?
you finished	you did not (didn't) finish	Did you finish?
he finished	he did not (didn't) finish	Did he finish?
she finished	she did not (didn't) finish	Did she finish?
it finished	it did not (didn't) finish	Did it finish?
we finished	we did not (didn't) finish	Did we finish?
you finished	you did not (didn't) finish	Did you finish?
they finished	they did not (didn't) finish	Did they finish?

Short answers

Yes, I/you did.	No, I/you didn't.
Yes, he/she/it did.	No, he/she/it didn't.
Yes, we/you/they did.	No, we/you/they didn't.

Past simple: irregular verbs

Affirmative	Negative	Question
I ate	I did not (didn't) eat	Did I eat?
you ate	you did not (didn't) eat	Did you eat?
he ate	he did not (didn't) eat	Did he eat?
she ate	she did not (didn't) eat	Did she eat?
it ate	it did not (didn't) eat	Did it eat?
we ate	we did not (didn't) eat	Did we eat?
you ate	you did not (didn't) eat	Did you eat?
they ate	they did not (didn't) eat	Did they eat?

When I was young, I didn't know how to drive. I used to walk everywhere.

Past simple and *used to* — Unit 2

Short answers

Yes, I/you did.   No, I/you didn't.
Yes, he/she/it did.   No, he/she/it didn't.
Yes, we/you/they did.   No, we/you/they didn't.

We use the past simple to talk about:

- things that started and finished in the past.
  He **visited** his aunt yesterday.
  I **lived** in London in 2012.

- things that happened often or were habits in the past.
  They **played** hockey when they were at school.
  My grandfather **rode** his bicycle to work every day.

- things that happened one after the other in the past.
  We **parked** the car, **got** our suitcases and **went** into the airport.
  He **got** dressed, **went** downstairs and **had** breakfast.

Notes

The *-ed* in the past simple is pronounced in three different ways.
-id, e.g. *wanted*
-t, e.g. *watched*
-d, e.g. *opened*

See the Irregular verbs list on page 164.

1 Make the sentences negative.

1 George knew how to get to York.
  George didn't know how to get to York.

2 Mum bought bread at the bakery.
  _____

3 The team played matches in Spain.
  _____

4 I ate three apples.
  _____

5 Emilia wrote an email to me.
  _____

2 Write questions.

1 When _____ did she leave _____ ?
  She left yesterday.

2 Who _____ ?
  I met Jenny.

3 Where _____ ?
  We saw them at the cinema.

4 Why _____ ?
  I said that because I was angry.

5 Where _____ ?
  I went to the beach.

6 How _____ ?
  I travelled to Italy by boat.

Unit 2 Past simple and *used to*

3 Write sentences. Use the verb in brackets.

1. My father wrote a book about computers. (read)
   My father didn't write a book about computers. He read a book about computers.
2. Carla sold a new pair of jeans. (buy)
   _____
3. My football team lost all their matches. (win)
   _____
4. The children walked to the park. (run)
   _____
5. We had a party. (go to)
   _____
6. We heard a bird in the garden. (see)
   _____

4 Complete the text with the past simple.

Last week, I saw a fantastic film. It ^{1} ___was___ (be) about how people ^{2} _____ (live) thousands of years ago. I ^{3} _____ (know) some of the things they ^{4} _____ (talk) about in the film, but I ^{5} _____ (not know) that life was so difficult. The men and women ^{6} _____ (do) lots of work. The men ^{7} _____ (hunt) for food, and the women ^{8} _____ (cook) the food and ^{9} _____ (make) clothes from animal skins. I'm glad I ^{10} _____ (not be) alive then!

Time expressions with the past simple

a month ago	last week
a week ago	last year
a year ago	on Sunday
in December	on 30th June
in 2015	the day before yesterday
last night	when I was five years old
last summer	yesterday

Time expressions come at the beginning or the end of a sentence.
*She went to the theatre **yesterday**.*
***Last year**, I travelled through Europe.*

Notes

When we talk about the past, we use the word *ago*, not the word *before*.
*I saw that film three days **ago**.*
*He worked here four years **ago**.*

Past simple and *used to* — Unit 2

5 Circle the words and expressions that go with the past simple.

(an hour ago)   in January   in 2008   last Saturday   next week   now   soon
tomorrow   when I'm older   years ago   yesterday

6 Now write sentences using the words or expressions from Exercise 5.
1 I arrived at school an hour ago.
2 _____
3 _____
4 _____
5 _____
6 _____

7 Write sentences using the past simple.
1 buy / a week ago / we / a lot of books for school
   We bought a lot of books for school a week ago.
2 break / the day before yesterday / her glasses / Ana
   _____
3 have / last week / you / a great party
   _____
4 Nadia / to her friend / on Monday / an email / send
   _____
5 be / last summer / very hot / it
   _____
6 some good music / hear / yesterday evening / on the radio / I
   _____

8 Complete the sentences with the past simple.
1 We ____watched____ (watch) TV until late last night.
2 _____ he _____ (find) his phone?
3 I _____ (not wake up) at seven o'clock on Sunday.
4 She _____ (not pay) to get into the cinema.
5 They _____ (see) a fantastic film last week.
6 What _____ she _____ (wear) to the party?
7 The show _____ (end) at eleven o'clock.
8 I _____ (hear) about the accident from my neighbour.
9 He _____ (travel) to Norway last winter.
10 She _____ (not go) shopping this morning.

Think about it!

The main verb does not change in the negative and question forms of the past simple.

15

Unit 2 — Past simple and *used to*

used to

Affirmative	Negative	Question
I used to play	I did not (didn't) use to play	Did I use to play?
you used to play	you did not (didn't) use to play	Did you use to play?
he used to play	he did not (didn't) use to play	Did he use to play?
she used to play	she did not (didn't) use to play	Did she use to play?
it used to play	it did not (didn't) use to play	Did it use to play?
we used to play	we did not (didn't) use to play	Did we use to play?
you used to play	you did not (didn't) use to play	Did you use to play?
they used to play	they did not (didn't) use to play	Did they use to play?

Short answers

Yes, I/you did.	No, I/you didn't.
Yes, he/she/it did.	No, he/she/it didn't.
Yes, we/you/they did.	No, we/you/they didn't.

We use *used to* to talk about:

- things that happened often in the past but that don't happen now.
  *I **used to** play a lot of sport, but now I don't.*
  *She **didn't use to** drive to work.*

- situations that existed in the past but that don't exist now.
  *She **used to** live in London, but now she lives in Paris.*

Notes

Be careful – the negative and question form is *use to*, not *used to*.

---

9 Complete the sentences with *used to* or *use to*.

1 Didn't you ____use to____ have brown hair?
2 I _____ walk to school every day, but now I ride my bike.
3 They didn't _____ live in a flat ten years ago, but now they do.
4 My sister _____ help me with my homework when I was ten years old.
5 Did you _____ watch children's programmes on TV?
6 Gordon didn't _____ to like classical music, but he does now.

10 Write questions.

1 You used to own ten pairs of shoes.
   <u>Did you use to own ten pairs of shoes?</u>
2 Stefan used to eat a lot of meat.
   _____
3 I used to play the violin when I was a child.
   _____
4 They used to play baseball on Wednesdays.
   _____
5 You used to write a lot of letters.
   _____
6 Elena used to go skiing when she was young.
   _____

Past simple and *used to* Unit 2

11 Complete the sentences with the correct form of *used to* and the verb in brackets.
1 I _____used to drink_____ (drink) milk, but now I prefer coffee.
2 Millions of years ago, dinosaurs _____ (live) on Earth.
3 Mum _____ (not like) eggs, but now she does.
4 _____ you _____ (read) comics when you were a boy?
5 He _____ (wear) a suit to work, but now he doesn't.
6 Television pictures _____ (be) in black and white.
7 We _____ (not send) emails, but now we do.
8 _____ the world _____ (be) colder millions of years ago?

12 Complete the sentences in your own words.
1 He lives in the countryside now,
   but _____he used to live in the city_____ .
2 I send emails to my friends,
   but _____ .
3 She wears T-shirts and jeans now,
   but _____ .
4 You don't like going to the park, but _____ .
5 We watch a lot of TV nowadays, but _____ .
6 He has got a lot of money now, but _____ .

Think about it!

Used to is followed by the infinitive (without *to*) of the main verb.

13 Circle the correct answer.
1 We __ every room in the house last week.
   a used to clean   b clean   (c) cleaned
2 My friend __ me a bag for my birthday.
   a gave   b used to give   c given
3 Did you __ live in France?
   a used to   b use   c use to
4 __ they know the shop was closed yesterday?
   a Use   b Did they use   c Did
5 Our teacher __ be a firefighter.
   a use to   b didn't used   c used to
6 I __ the shopping early this morning.
   a used to   b did   c do
7 __ she use to buy her clothes in London?
   a Did   b Was   c Used
8 Thousands of years ago, people __ in caves.
   a used to live   b used to   c live

17

Unit 2 Past simple and *used to*

14 **Find the mistakes in the sentences. Then write them correctly.**

1 I <u>lose</u> my watch yesterday.
   I lost my watch yesterday.

2 We use to live on a farm.
   _____

3 Did you saw the documentary about kangaroos last night?
   _____

4 What did you used to eat when you were four years old?
   _____

5 Do you eat your dinner at eight o'clock yesterday?
   _____

6 I use to enjoy watching gymnastics on TV.
   _____

7 She didn't knew what to buy her friend for her birthday.
   _____

8 What time he came to school this morning?
   _____

15 **Match 1–6 with a–f. Then write sentences.**

1 They played   a to watch TV in black and white?
2 Did you live   b to like cycling. He loves it now!
3 Did people use   c live in Scotland.
4 What time did you   d chess for two hours last night.
5 We used to   e get up last Sunday?
6 He didn't use   f in England when you were younger?

1 They played chess for two hours last night.
2 _____
3 _____
4 _____
5 _____
6 _____

Past simple and *used to* — Unit 2

16 **Tick (✓) the correct sentence, *a* or *b*.**

1. a I eated pizza and ice cream at my birthday party. ___
   b I ate pizza and ice cream at my birthday party. ✓
2. a Did your grandparents use to listen to pop music? ___
   b Did your grandparents used to listen to pop music? ___
3. a Juan arrived home at nine o'clock last night. ___
   b Juan used to arrive home at nine o'clock last night. ___
4. a Did you buy that bracelet from the new shop in town? ___
   b Did you bought that bracelet from the new shop in town? ___
5. a How did they used to made clothes thousands of years ago? ___
   b How did they make clothes thousands of years ago? ___
6. a Did your father used to be a singer? ___
   b Did your father use to be a singer? ___
7. a What time did he come to school this morning? ___
   b What time he came to school this morning? ___
8. a Did he remember his mother's birthday? ___
   b Did he remembered his mother's birthday? ___

Pairwork

Work in pairs. Tell your partner three things which you did yesterday. Tell your partner three things which you used to do but you don't do now.

Writing

1. Write a short paragraph about what you did last weekend.

2. Write a short paragraph about what life was like in your town fifty years ago.

UNIT 3
Past continuous and past simple

Past continuous

Affirmative	Negative	Question
I was sleeping	I was not (wasn't) sleeping	Was I sleeping?
you were sleeping	you were not (weren't) sleeping	Were you sleeping?
he was sleeping	he was not (wasn't) sleeping	Was he sleeping?
she was sleeping	she was not (wasn't) sleeping	Was she sleeping?
it was sleeping	it was not (wasn't) sleeping	Was it sleeping?
we were sleeping	we were not (weren't) sleeping	Were we sleeping?
you were sleeping	you were not (weren't) sleeping	Were you sleeping?
they were sleeping	they were not (weren't) sleeping	Were they sleeping?

Short answers	
Yes, I was.	No, I wasn't.
Yes, you were.	No, you weren't.
Yes, he/she/it was.	No, he/she/it wasn't.
Yes, we/you/they were.	No, we/you/they weren't.

We use the past continuous:

- to talk about actions that were in progress at a particular time in the past.
  I **was writing** an email at five o'clock yesterday afternoon.
  They **were travelling** to the US last Saturday.

- to talk about two or more actions that were in progress at the same time in the past.
  He **was washing** the car and **listening** to the radio.
  Mum **was making** lunch and Dad **was gardening**.

- for setting the scene of a story.
  The sun **was shining** and the birds **were singing** in the trees.
  The wind **was blowing** and it **was raining**.

I was walking in the park when it started to rain.

Past continuous and past simple — Unit 3

1 Make the sentences negative.

1 They were waiting for Pietro outside the library.
 They weren't waiting for Pietro outside the library.
2 I was thinking about my friends.
 _____
3 He was looking for his phone.
 _____
4 We were walking for a long time.
 _____
5 Sofia was working on her computer at seven o'clock.
 _____

Think about it!

The past continuous has got three parts:
– the subject pronoun (I, you, he, etc.);
– the verb to be (was or were);
– the main verb with an -ing ending.

2 Write questions.

1 He was looking in the wrong place for his keys.
 Was he looking in the wrong place for his keys?
2 They were waiting outside the cinema for an hour.
 _____
 _____
3 You were learning Spanish last year.
 _____
 _____
4 Leon was talking to Lisa during the English lesson.
 _____
 _____
5 It was snowing yesterday.
 _____
 _____
6 They were wearing smart clothes last weekend.
 _____
 _____

3 Complete the sentences with the past continuous.

1 The neighbours _were playing_ (play) music and I _was trying_ (try) to sleep.
2 The musicians _____ (practise) for the concert all week.
3 She _____ (swim) in the sea yesterday afternoon.
4 Who _____ (drive) the car – you or your father?
5 I _____ (work) very hard all evening.
6 The children _____ (tidy) the kitchen and Dad _____ (do) the washing up.
7 The sky was dark and the wind _____ (blow).
8 Hamid _____ (study) all day yesterday.

Unit 3 — Past continuous and past simple

Past continuous and past simple

We use the past continuous and the past simple together when:

- one action in the past interrupts another action in the past.
  I **was sleeping** when the phone **rang**.
  They **were eating** lunch when we **arrived**.

- we tell a story in the past.
  We **were watching** TV when we **heard** a loud noise outside. We **opened** the door and a man **was standing** there **wearing** a tall black hat and a coat.

when and while

We use *when* with the past simple.
When I got home, my friends were waiting for me.
She was eating her dinner **when I arrived**.

We use *while* with the past continuous.
While I was working, Dad **was making** lunch.
It **was raining while I was sleeping**.

4 Complete the sentences with the past continuous or past simple.

1. The sun __was shining__ (shine) and the birds __were singing__ (sing) when I __woke up__ (wake up) this morning.
2. What _____ you _____ (do) when I _____ (phone) you?
3. I _____ (make) a pizza when Mum _____ (come) home.
4. When I _____ (go) to town, it _____ (rain).
5. He _____ (drive) too fast when the accident _____ (happen).
6. While I _____ (walk) home, it _____ (start) to rain.

5 Complete the sentences with *when* or *while*.

1. The children were laughing ____while____ they were watching the funny film.
2. He wasn't very happy _____ I arrived late.
3. _____ Yulia was making lunch, her children were playing in the garden.
4. I was so sorry _____ I heard about your accident.
5. _____ we went to London, the weather was cold and wet.
6. I was reading _____ Omar was talking on the phone.
7. Jenny was working on her computer _____ the electricity went off.
8. _____ the train reached the station, we were having coffee in the café.

Past continuous and past simple — Unit 3

6 Write questions.

1 Who / she talk to / on the phone / when / I arrive / ?
   Who was she talking to on the phone when I arrived?
2 Where / you play tennis / yesterday afternoon / ?
   _____
   _____
3 Who / you dance with / at the party / last Saturday / ?
   _____
   _____
4 What / your dad listen to / while / he / cook / ?
   _____
   _____
5 What / the children do / when / their mum / come home / ?
   _____
   _____
6 What / your friends wear / when / you see them / ?
   _____
   _____

7 Complete the sentences with the past simple or past continuous.

1 While he __was driving__ (drive) along the road, a dog ____ran____ (run) in front of his car.
2 They _____ (ski) in Austria when their instructor _____ (break) his leg.
3 I _____ (study) in my bedroom when Mum _____ (call) me.
4 While the clothes _____ (dry) on the line, the wind _____ (blow).
5 _____ (you / have) a bath when I _____ (phone)?
6 While I _____ (work) on the computer, Dan _____ (do) the washing up.

8 Complete the sentences in your own words.

1 When I woke up this morning, __the sun was shining__ .
2 While I was travelling to town, _____
   _____ .
3 When I finished my lunch, _____
   _____ .
4 What were you doing when _____
   _____ ?
5 It was raining while _____
   _____ .
6 While Mum was driving, _____
   _____ .
7 Jan was watching TV when _____
   _____ .
8 The baby was sleeping while _____
   _____ .

23

Unit 3   Past continuous and past simple

9 Circle the correct answers.
1. I *was dreaming* / *dreamt* when the alarm clock *was waking* / *woke* me up.
2. I *was sitting* / *sat* in the garden when the rain *was starting* / *started*.
3. What *were you doing* / *did you do* when I *was seeing* / *saw* you yesterday?
4. The boys *played* / *were playing* football when Gregory *had* / *was having* his accident.
5. Dad *cooked* / *was cooking* in the kitchen when Mum *was getting* / *got* home.
6. When my favourite programme *started* / *was starting*, I *was did* / *was doing* my homework.
7. The girls *were eating* / *ate* spaghetti when Billy *was taking* / *took* their photograph.
8. When the lights *went* / *were going* out, we *were thinking* / *thought* it was an earthquake.

Think about it!

Always think about which of the two actions took a long time and which happened quickly. Use the past continuous for the longer action and the past simple for the short action.

10 Find the mistakes in the sentences. Then write them correctly.
1. While I was doing my homework, I suddenly <u>was hearing</u> a loud noise.
   <u>While I was doing my homework, I suddenly heard a loud noise.</u>
2. They were sitting on the beach when a huge wave was coming and covered them in water.
   _____
3. I wrote an email to my best friend when the computer broke down.
   _____
4. My sister was practising the cello while I studied history.
   _____
5. The wind was blowing hard when the trees were falling down.
   _____
6. Were you playing the drums when I was phoning you?
   _____

11 Complete the text with the past simple or the past continuous.

One day, while I ¹ <u>was walking</u> (walk) along the road, I ² _____ (see) an old lady. She ³ _____ (wear) a bright purple coat and a large black hat, and she ⁴ _____ (carry) a parrot in a cage. She ⁵ _____ (look) very unusual and I ⁶ _____ (not want) to talk to her, but she ⁷ _____ (smile) at me and asked me the time. I ⁸ _____ (tell) her the time and she said she ⁹ _____ (be) late for an important meeting. Then she ¹⁰ _____ (ask) me the quickest way to get to Buckingham Palace! While I was thinking what a strange person she was, she ¹¹ _____ (disappear) completely. I ¹² _____ (think) it was a dream, but then I saw a red parrot feather on the ground by my foot!

Past continuous and past simple — Unit 3

12 Match 1–6 with a–f. Then write sentences.

1 Who was he jogging with when
2 What were they
3 Mum went to the shops and
4 What were you doing
5 Dad was playing golf
6 While we were staying in London,

a while I was cleaning the house.
b she bought a new dress.
c he fell and broke his ankle?
d we went to the Tower of London.
e watching on TV when you arrived?
f when the storm started?

1 Who was he jogging with when he fell and broke his ankle?
2 _____
3 _____
4 _____
5 _____
6 _____

Pairwork

Work in pairs. Take turns to ask and answer the questions below.

- What were you doing at eight o'clock yesterday evening?
- What was happening in your house at seven o'clock this morning?
- What was the weather like when you woke up this morning?
- What was everybody in your family doing last Saturday morning?
- What was everybody in your family wearing yesterday?

Writing

Write a paragraph describing a thunderstorm. Imagine you were out in the storm. Think about the points below.

- the weather
- what was happening around you
- what happened to the trees, the roads, the animals, the sky and your clothes
- how you felt and what you did

UNIT 4
Present perfect simple

Present perfect simple

Affirmative	Negative	Question
I have (I've) finished	I have not (haven't) finished	Have I finished?
you have (you've) finished	you have not (haven't) finished	Have you finished?
he has (he's) finished	he has not (hasn't) finished	Has he finished?
she has (she's) finished	she has not (hasn't) finished	Has she finished?
it has (it's) finished	it has not (hasn't) finished	Has it finished?
we have (we've) finished	we have not (haven't) finished	Have we finished?
you have (you've) finished	you have not (haven't) finished	Have you finished?
they have (they've) finished	they have not (haven't) finished	Have they finished?

Short answers

Yes, I/you have.	No, I/you haven't.
Yes, he/she/it has.	No, he/she/it hasn't.
Yes, we/you/they have.	No, we/you/they haven't.

The present perfect simple is formed with the verb *have/has* and the past participle of the main verb. See the Irregular verbs list on page 164.

We use the present perfect simple to talk about:

- something that happened in the past but we don't know exactly when.
  They **have seen** this film.
  She **has** already **had** her lunch.

- something that happened in the past but has a connection with the present.
  He **has packed** all his things, so he's ready to leave.
  I **have lost** my keys. I can't open the front door.

- something that started in the past but has not finished.
  I **have worked** in this company since 2015.
  It **has been** hot for a week.

- something that just happened.
  We **have** just **finished** painting the house.
  He **has** just **washed** the car.

I've never done a skydive before!

Present perfect simple Unit 4

1 Complete the sentences with the present perfect simple.

1 The students __have finished__ (finish) their science projects.
2 We _____ (miss) the bus, so we're walking home.
3 My father _____ (travel) to many different countries.
4 I _____ (eat) all my food.
5 She _____ (send) all her emails.
6 I _____ (find) the book you wanted.
7 The weather _____ (be) great this week.
8 They _____ (forget) where they put their coats.

Think about it!

Remember to use the past participle of the main verb.

2 Make the sentences negative.

1 I have finished my work.
   I haven't finished my work.
2 I have seen the Statue of Liberty.
   _____
3 She has washed her car.
   _____
4 They have been friends for ages.
   _____
5 Mum has bought strawberries.
   _____
6 Miguel has studied in France.
   _____

3 Write questions.

1 He has won the race.
   Has he won the race?
2 They have gone to the cinema.
   _____
3 You have been to Italy.
   _____
4 He has washed his hair.
   _____
5 Kim has done her homework.
   _____
6 The teacher has explained everything.
   _____

4 Write answers using the verb in brackets.

1 Has he made the pizza? (eat)
   No, he hasn't. He has eaten the pizza.
2 Have you broken your new pen? (lose)
   _____
3 Has your dad driven to Portugal? (fly)
   _____
4 Has Marco dried his hair? (wash)
   _____
5 Have astronauts visit the planet Mars? (study)
   _____
6 Has she failed the exam? (pass)
   _____

27

Unit 4 Present perfect simple

Time expressions with the present perfect simple

already	never
ever	since
for	yet
just	

She's **already** had lunch./Has she **already** had lunch?
Have you **ever** visited Egypt?
We've lived here **for** six years.
I've **just** finished my homework.
I've **never** met a famous person.
We've been married **since** 2009.
He hasn't done the shopping **yet**./Has he done the shopping **yet**?

Notes

We use **for** with a period of time (**for** two years, **for** many hours) and **since** with a specific point in time (**since** 2016, **since** I was a baby).

5 Complete the sentences with *yet* or *already*.

1 I haven't finished my breakfast ____yet____ .
2 They haven't had their exam results _____ .
3 I've _____ tidied my room.
4 Have you made your bed _____ ?
5 I haven't brushed my teeth _____ .
6 Dad has _____ done the shopping.
7 The bank manager hasn't lent me any money _____ .
8 The children have _____ gone to bed.
9 I've _____ seen that film.
10 Have you _____ done your homework?

6 Complete the sentences with *for* or *since*.

1 He's worked in that shop ____for____ five years.
2 I've studied English _____ I was eight years old.
3 Have you had that toy _____ you were a baby?
4 We've been trying to do this exercise _____ a long time.
5 I haven't seen my cousin _____ two months.
6 My grammar has improved _____ I started trying harder.
7 We've known each other _____ ten years.
8 They've had that car _____ 2018.

7 Rewrite the sentences with *have* or *has* in the correct place.

1 Those boys just bought a new tent.
   Those boys have just bought a new tent.

2 He already finished his homework.

3 Lin made lunch yet?

4 They lived in Paris since their child was born.

5 I never been to the US.

6 We just eaten our breakfast.

28

Present perfect simple   Unit 4

8 Write sentences. Use the verb in brackets.

1. Mum used to go to work by bus. Now she drives to work. (buy)
   Mum has bought a car.
2. Dad isn't at the office now. (leave)
   _____
3. He was playing football and now he can't walk. (break)
   _____
4. The train leaves at eight o'clock, and it's half past eight now. (miss)
   _____
5. I put my phone on the table, but it isn't there now. (lose)
   _____
6. It's my birthday, but my friend hasn't bought me a present. (forget)
   _____

9 Complete the sentences with the words from the box.

| already | for | has | ~~have~~ | never | remembered | tried | yet |

1. They ___have___ been to New Zealand lots of times.
2. I have _____ to learn Russian, but it's difficult.
3. _____ he given you some money for food?
4. I haven't read this book _____ .
5. We've _____ seen that film. Can we watch a different one?
6. Has Dad _____ that it's Mum's birthday today?
7. I've worked in this bank _____ five years.
8. They've _____ seen an eclipse.

have been and have gone

We use *have been* to say that someone went somewhere and came back. They have experience of something.
I **have been** to the US. It was fantastic!
Have you **been** to the new Italian restaurant?

We use *have gone* to say that someone went somewhere and is still there.
Penny is not here. She **has gone** to the bank.
It's very quiet in the house. **Have** the children **gone** to school?

10 Complete the sentences with *have/has been* or *have/has gone*.

1. I ___have___ never ___been___ on an aeroplane before.
2. 'Where _____ Aliya _____?' 'She is at the supermarket.'
3. Alex _____ in hospital, but he is better now.
4. I'm ill, so my friends _____ to the cinema without me.
5. They waited for you for two hours, and now they _____ home.
6. _____ you ever _____ to Canada?

29

Unit 4 Present perfect simple

11 Find the extra word and write it in the space.

1 What have they to done with their old clothes? _____to_____
2 I've have already seen that film. _____
3 The programme about dinosaurs has finished yet. _____
4 Has he written since to his uncle in Australia? _____
5 I've lived here since I was for three. _____
6 We've just worked hard this week. _____
7 The volcano has erupted yet and the local people have left their homes. _____
8 I have ever seen the Tower of London. _____

12 Find the mistakes in the sentences. Then write them correctly.

1 How long was she been a police officer?
  How long has she been a police officer?
2 We've eat all the biscuits.
  _____
3 Has they used all the milk?
  _____
4 Have you ever gone to Egypt?
  _____
5 I've ever done a parachute jump.
  _____
6 The baby has fell asleep.
  _____

13 Write the words in the correct order.

1 gone / has / university / to / your / yet / brother / ?
  Has your brother gone to university yet?
2 our / booked / we / yet / holiday / haven't
  _____
3 already / she / her / has / room / tidied
  _____
4 with / what / pen / you / done / have / my / ?
  _____
5 the / for / they / party / lots of / bought / food / have
  _____
6 already / waited / we / have / three / for / hours
  _____

Present perfect simple — Unit 4

14 Match 1–6 with a–f. Then write sentences.

1 Have you ever   a I've broken my leg.
2 I can't do gymnastics because   b eaten their dinner yet?
3 The teacher has given   c visited Buckingham Palace?
4 Have they   d for years.
5 I've already   e us a lot of homework.
6 I've had these jeans   f made lunch.

1 Have you ever visited Buckingham Palace?
2 _____
3 _____
4 _____
5 _____
6 _____

15 Complete the sentences in your own words.

1 I have never _____ seen a zebra in the wild _____.
2 I have seen _____.
3 My friend has just _____.
4 My teacher has already _____.
5 I have been to _____.
6 Have you ever _____?

Pairwork

Work in pairs. Using the present perfect simple, take turns to ask and answer about the activities below.

- visit Paris
- see the Giza Pyramids
- eat Japanese food
- read a play by William Shakespeare
- dye your hair
- wear pink trousers
- lose a lot of money
- win a competition

Writing

1 Write a list of the things you have and haven't done during the last two months.

2 Write a list of the things you have never done but would like to do.

Grammar review 1 — Units 1–4

1 Complete the sentences with do, does, am, is or are.

1 ____Do____ you have any brothers or sisters?
2 Where _____ you and your brother live?
3 _____ he listen carefully to the English teacher?
4 I _____ listening to everything he says, but I don't understand it all!
5 _____ the computer working properly?
6 _____ you busy at the moment?
7 What _____ the email say?
8 _____ I interrupting your conversation?

2 Complete the sentences with the present simple or present continuous.

1 ____Are____ you ____using____ (use) your computer at the moment?
2 She _____ (not know) how to speak English.
3 I always _____ (take) an umbrella with me when I go out.
4 He _____ (live) in a hotel until he finds a flat.
5 Today we _____ (learn) about the environment.
6 _____ he _____ (want) a new laptop for his birthday?
7 My cousin _____ (stay) with us this week.
8 It usually _____ (get) cold in the winter.

3 Circle the correct answer.

1 I don't like cherries. I __ strawberries.
  a am preferring   (b) prefer   c do prefer
2 He __ the teacher a lot of questions today.
  a asks   b doesn't ask   c is asking
3 Where does she __ to go at the weekend?
  a wants   b want   c wanting
4 He __ English very well.
  a understands   b is understanding
  c understand
5 Sometimes we __ to school.
  a walking   b walks   c walk
6 What __ in your house at the moment?
  a is happening   b does happen   c happens
7 I __ eggs for breakfast every day.
  a eats   b am eating   c eat
8 __ you watching this programme or shall I turn it off?
  a Do   b Have   c Are

4 Complete the sentences with the words from the box.

| always | at | every | in |
| never | now | on | ~~twice~~ |

1 I brush my teeth ____twice____ a day.
2 He listens to music _____ day.
3 Lisa studies English _____ the weekend.
4 Mum _____ kisses the baby goodnight.
5 The rain is stopping _____ , so we can go out.
6 Aida goes to her music lesson _____ Saturday mornings.
7 He is very honest and _____ tells lies.
8 My grandmother sits by the fire and reads her book _____ the evenings.

Units 1–4   **Grammar review 1**

5 Complete the sentences with the past simple.
1 I _____forgot_____ (forget) to give him the message!
2 I _____ (not think) the film was very interesting.
3 _____ they _____ (buy) ice creams for everyone?
4 We _____ (not know) all the answers in the test.
5 You _____ (be) late for school again yesterday.
6 Karen _____ (get) a new T-shirt and a pair of jeans for her birthday.
7 _____ he _____ (realise) it was snowing when he got up?
8 Dad _____ (do) the washing up last night.
9 She was angry because Emil _____ (come) home late.
10 He _____ (drink) all the milk and now there is none left.

6 Circle the correct answer.
1 There didn't __ to be any electricity on this island.
   a used   b *use*   c be used
2 Did you __ go to school by bus?
   a used   b used to   c use to
3 We all __ shopping last Saturday.
   a went   b used to go   c did go
4 Where __ his mother meet his father?
   a did   b used to   c was
5 He __ bring me a souvenir from London.
   a wasn't   b used   c didn't
6 Dad __ play football when he was young.
   a used to   b didn't to   c use to
7 __ he use to get into trouble when he was at school?
   a Did   b Was   c Used
8 I __ my cousins three weeks ago.
   a used to see   b see   c saw

7 Circle the correct answer.
1 They moved to Australia *last* / *ago* year.
2 My brother used to eat a lot of sweets *when* / *as* he was young.
3 What games did people use to play hundreds of years *before* / *ago*?
4 Did all the students do their homework *yesterday* / *last day*?
5 She started her last job *in* / *at* 2017.
6 *Two days ago* / *Before two days* she flew to America.
7 I'm tired because I worked until very late *yesterday night* / *last night*.
8 I got up very late *before* / *yesterday*.

Grammar review 1 — Units 1–4

8 Complete the sentences with the past continuous.

1 They _were waiting_ (wait) for the bus for half an hour.
2 _____ he _____ (run) around the track all morning?
3 The leaves _____ (fall) off the tree last week.
4 It _____ (rain) all day yesterday.
5 I _____ (make) lunch an hour ago.
6 _____ the professor _____ (speak) on the phone all morning?
7 We _____ (do) our homework for three hours this afternoon.
8 Mary _____ (not listen) to the teacher.

9 Circle the correct answer.

1 I *had* / *was having* a shower when the phone rang.
2 *Was* / *Were* he fishing while you were swimming?
3 They *walked* / *were walk* to the beach yesterday.
4 When *did* / *was* he start to speak English?
5 It *was* / *was being* hot when we arrived at the airport.
6 He *was talking* / *was talked* all afternoon.
7 What was your father doing when your mother *arrived* / *was arriving* home?
8 The cats *sleep* / *were sleeping* while the dogs were barking.

10 Write sentences. Use the past simple, past continuous and *when*, *while* or *and* to join the two parts.

1 she cycle to town / fall off her bicycle
   She was cycling to town when she fell off her bicycle.

2 I do the washing up / I break a glass
   _____
   _____

3 she listen to music / I arrive
   _____
   _____

4 the sun shine / I lie in the garden
   _____
   _____

5 the computer break down / I use it
   _____
   _____

6 you talk to someone in town / I see you
   _____
   _____

7 first she do the shopping / then she make a cake
   _____
   _____

8 Mariam play football / break her leg
   _____
   _____

Units 1–4   Grammar review 1

11 Rewrite the second sentence with a similar meaning to the first. Use the word in brackets.

1 I saw Angela last week. (since)
   I haven't ___seen Angela since___ last week.

2 We gave them a lot of chocolate and they ate it all. (have)
   They _____ all the chocolate we gave them.

3 This is the best book I have ever read. (never)
   I _____ such a good book.

4 He can't find his keys. (lost)
   He _____ his keys.

5 Lucas bought a new motorcycle yesterday. (just)
   Lucas _____ a new motorcycle.

6 Ana is at the doctor's. (has)
   Ana _____ to the doctor's.

7 I must work for another two hours. (finished)
   I _____ my work yet.

8 I met Maria in 2017. (known)
   I _____ 2017.

12 Complete the sentences with the words from the box.

| already | always | ever | for | just | never |
| since | ~~yet~~ | | | | |

1 Have you done your homework ___yet___ ?
2 Don't make lunch. I've _____ made something.
3 I haven't seen you _____ ages.
4 The film has _____ finished.
5 Have you _____ eaten vegan food?
6 They've lived there _____ 2010.
7 Astronauts have _____ wanted to fly to Mars.
8 We've _____ been to China or India.

13 Find the extra word and write it in the space.

1 We've already eaten yet, so we aren't hungry now. ___yet___
2 Have you lived here since you were for born? _____
3 They have to seen the Acropolis. _____
4 Have you ever been wanted to go to Australia? _____
5 The holiday it has been really brilliant! _____
6 Have you ever did been to Holland? _____
7 Who has travelled abroad since this year? _____
8 Eva has always bought some cherries for you. _____
9 Has he remembered to bring his mobile phone already? _____
10 What has she did promised to do? _____

UNIT 5
Past simple and present perfect simple

Past simple

I finished my homework an hour ago.
You didn't finish your homework an hour ago.
Did she finish her homework an hour ago?

I bought a new coat.
You didn't buy a new coat.
Did he buy a new coat?

We use the past simple to talk about:

- something that happened at a specified time in the past.
  James **lost** his keys yesterday.
  Shazia **phoned** her sister this morning.

- something that started and finished in the past.
  They **moved** into this house four years ago.
  She **went** to Spain last year.

1 Complete the sentences with the past simple.

1 _____Did_____ you _____see_____ (see) the paintings by Picasso in the art gallery?
2 Where _____ (be) you when I called at your house?
3 He _____ (have) a shower at six o'clock.
4 I _____ (find) a wallet on my way to school this morning.
5 They _____ (not know) the answers to all the questions in the exam.
6 Tom _____ (finish) his project last week.
7 They _____ (visit) their grandparents in Cornwall last summer.
8 The manager _____ (not go) to the meeting because he was very busy.

Past simple and present perfect simple — Unit 5

Present perfect simple

I have cleaned the car.
You haven't cleaned the car.
Has he cleaned the car?

I have drunk all the milk.
You haven't drunk all the milk.
Has she drunk all the milk?

We use the present perfect simple to talk about:

- something that happened in the past but we don't know when.
  I**'ve been** to Finland.
  She**'s lost** her English book.

- something that started and finished in the past but is still important now.
  I **have broken** my leg, so I can't walk.
  His car **has broken down**, so he can't take us to the airport.

- something that started in the past but hasn't finished yet.
  I **have worked** here for two years.
  She **has lived** in Manchester since she was born.

2 Complete the sentences with the present perfect simple.

1 We __have bought__ (buy) a new flat in Edinburgh.
2 He _____ (think) of a new way to earn money.
3 Scientists _____ (find) a way to make people live longer.
4 Astronauts _____ (discover) some new stars.
5 I _____ (not eat) all my lunch because I don't feel well.
6 _____ he _____ (hear) from his friend since he went back to the US?
7 Eric _____ (break) his glasses. Now he can't see properly.
8 _____ you ever _____ (travel) to the Alps?

Think about it!

We use the past participle of the main verb for all forms of the present perfect simple.

3 Write *PS* if the verb is in the past simple and *PPS* is the verb is in the present perfect simple.

1 He went to the gym every day last week.
   ____PS____
2 They had a picnic in the forest last Saturday.
   _____
3 I've had too much to eat. _____
4 Did you have a good time at the party? _____
5 Has he seen his new bicycle yet? _____
6 We've visited lots of countries in Europe.
   _____
7 They didn't have cereal for breakfast. _____
8 I played volleyball this morning. _____

Unit 5 — Past simple and present perfect simple

4 Write sentences with the past simple or present perfect simple.

1. Nina / go / China / last year
   Nina went to China last year.
2. She / never / see / a giraffe
   _____
3. He / go / to the gym / yesterday
   _____
4. I / be / to the theatre / twice this year
   _____
5. Astronauts / land / on the moon / in 1969
   _____
6. Lee / know / how to speak Russian / since he was six
   _____

5 Write questions.

1. Has he ever flown in a plane?
   No, he's never flown in a plane.
2. _____
   Yes, I waited for my mum outside the supermarket.
3. _____
   Yes, I've revised for all my exams.
4. _____
   No, she didn't know the party was on Saturday.
5. _____
   Yes, the car broke down when we were on the motorway.
6. _____
   Yes, I saw my friends in town.

6 Complete the sentences with the past simple or present perfect simple.

1. Last month, I ____fell____ (fall) in the garden and I __have walked__ (walk) with a stick since then.
2. I _____ (know) Jenny since we _____ (be) at school together.
3. I _____ (send) my friend two emails this week, but she _____ (not reply) yet.
4. _____ (you / cut) your hair since the last time I _____ (see) you?
5. We _____ (make) a cake for Mum's birthday already, but we _____ (not buy) her present yet.
6. I _____ (be) to see the doctor twice since Monday, but she _____ (say) there is nothing wrong with me.

7 Circle the correct answer.

1. I've *never* / *ever* noticed that building before.
2. She *knew* / *has known* him for ten years.
3. I *haven't* / *didn't* finished yet.
4. Did you *seen* / *see* the documentary about Africa on TV last night?
5. I *ate* / *have eaten* my lunch before I went shopping.
6. Has he *meet* / *met* the new student from Bulgaria?
7. We have known Jim *since* / *for* 2016.
8. Has she ever *been* / *went* to Asia?

Past simple and present perfect simple — Unit 5

8 Look at the table and write sentences.

Fifteen years ago	Today
only drink milk	drink coffee and tea
like soft food	eat Chinese and Indian food
play with dolls	become good at chess
not work	work in a shop and a café
speak English	learn French
wear flowery skirts	buy jeans and T-shirts
listen to nursery rhymes	hear lots of rock music

1   When Melanie was five, she only drank milk. Since turning twenty, she has drunk tea and coffee.
2   ____
3   ____
4   ____
5   ____
6   ____
7   ____

9 Complete the sentences with the words from the box.

> ago   for   has   last week   ~~never~~   since   speak   spoken

1   We've _____never_____ eaten Polish food.
2   _____ he read all those computer magazines yet?
3   Did you _____ English when you were four years old?
4   They moved into a new flat two months _____ .
5   Have you _____ to the teacher about this exercise?
6   We've lived in Japan _____ 2017.
7   I met Valerie _____ .
8   She's driven a jeep _____ two years.

Unit 5 — Past simple and present perfect simple

10 Find the mistakes in the sentences. Then write them correctly.

1 I've never woke up so late before.
   I've never woken up so late before.

2 When you been small, did you like olives?
   _____

3 Has you ever been to Brazil?
   _____

4 They've did built a new library since I moved here.
   _____

5 I've wanted to visit India for I was a child.
   _____

6 What have you do when you were at the park?
   _____

11 Find the extra word and write it in the space.

1 He's just eaten a huge pizza yet.
   _____yet_____

2 Has your team did won all their matches this season? _____

3 Lots of animals they have died in the forest fire. _____

4 When since did you break your arm? _____

5 Did you go to school when you have were four years old? _____

6 I've did forgotten your name. _____

7 What has been happened since I left you alone this morning? _____

8 Our neighbours have came back from their holiday with sunburn. _____

12 Circle the correct answer.

1 The train has ___ arrived at the station.
   (a) just   b yet   c ever

2 We ___ to watch the football cup final.
   a been   b have went
   c have been

3 We've ___ asked the teacher about the things we don't understand.
   a ever   b yet   c already

4 ___ you go to the cinema last night?
   a Have   b Did   c Were

5 He never ___ eggs when he was young.
   a has eaten   b ate   c did eat

6 How long ___ known about this?
   a did you   b have   c have you

13 Circle the correct answer.

1 Julia has had blonde hair (since)/ when she was eighteen.

2 Where did they go on holiday *last* / *before* summer?

3 Did you know Bill two years *ago* / *since*?

4 Kareem has *ever* / *just* been snowboarding.

5 My computer hasn't worked *since* / *for* weeks.

6 I've *never* / *already* liked junk food.

7 I haven't been to Italy *when* / *since* I was a young boy.

8 Have you *always* / *already* wanted to ride a motorbike?

Past simple and present perfect simple — Unit 5

14 Complete the sentences in your own words.

1 Since 2015, I have _____ learnt how to speak Italian _____ .
2 Last year, I _____ .
3 I _____ for two years.
4 When I was eight I _____ .
5 Last weekend, I _____ ,
   but since then I _____ .
6 Last year, I _____ , and since then
   I _____ .

Pairwork

Work in pairs. Using the past simple and the present perfect simple, take turns to ask and answer the questions below.

- When did you have your first English lesson?
- How long have you lived in the house you live in now?
- What did you do last night?
- Have you ever been to another country?
- Where did you go for your holidays last summer?
- Have you ever cooked a meal for your family?
- What did you eat for lunch yesterday?
- What music have you listened to this week?
- What TV programmes have you watched this week?

Writing

Write a letter to your friend telling him/her about something that has happened to you recently. Think about the points below and include verbs in the past simple and the present perfect simple in your letter.

- Is it something happy, exciting, unusual, dangerous or funny?
- Is it somewhere you visited?
- Is it someone you have met?

Dear _____ ,

_____
_____
_____
_____
_____

Love from,

_____

UNIT 6

Future tenses

I'm going to learn to water ski! I'm having my first lesson in half an hour.

Great! I'll watch you.

Present continuous: future meaning

I am having a party next Saturday. Is he coming to the cinema with us tonight?
You are not leaving tomorrow.

We can use the present continuous to talk about plans and arrangements for the future.
We're meeting him outside the restaurant later.
They are going to their grandmother's house tomorrow.

Jemma's diary

Monday:	clean house
Tuesday:	make cake
Wednesday:	do shopping
Thursday:	exercise at gym
Friday:	wash hair
Saturday:	get married!
Sunday:	go on honeymoon!

1 Write sentences.

1 _She's cleaning the house on Monday._
2 _____
3 _____
4 _____
5 _____
6 _____
7 _____

42

Future tenses — Unit 6

Future simple

Affirmative	Negative	Question
I will (I'll) work	I will not (won't) work	Will/Shall I work?
you will (you'll) work	you will not (won't) work	Will you work?
he will (he'll) work	he will not (won't) work	Will he work?
she will (she'll) work	she will not (won't) work	Will she work?
it will (it'll) work	it will not won't) work	Will it work?
we will (we'll) work	we will not (won't) work	Will/Shall we work?
you will (you'll) work	you will not (won't) work	Will you work?
they will (they'll) work	they will not (won't) work	Will they work?

Short answers

Yes, I/you will.   No, I/you won't.
Yes, he/she/it will.   No, he/she/it won't.
Yes, we/you/they will.   No, we/you/they won't.

We use the future simple:

- for predictions for the future.
  *We **will drive** flying cars in the future.*

- for decisions made at the time of speaking.
  *This dress is perfect! I**'ll buy** it.*

- for promises.
  *I **won't be** late. I promise.*

- to offer to do something for someone.
  ***Shall** I **help** you with that?*
  *I**'ll take** you to the airport if you like.*

- for threats and warnings.
  *You**'ll fall** out of that tree.*

Notes

We use *shall* with *I* and *we* in questions when we want to offer to do something or when we are suggesting something.
***Shall** I get you a cup of coffee?*
***Shall** we have lunch together?*

---

2 Complete the sentences with the future simple.

1. He ___will be___ (be) the best footballer in the school when he's older.
2. We _____ (help) you to move house the day after tomorrow.
3. I _____ (carry) the shopping home for you.
4. My friend _____ (have) a coffee and a doughnut, and I _____ (have) a milkshake, please.
5. They _____ (look) really nice in their new clothes.
6. I _____ (come) home before it gets dark.
7. Don't worry. You _____ (pass) your driving test.
8. _____ I _____ (help) you with the cooking?

> **Think about it!**
>
> The future simple is very easy! Just remember to add *will* (or *shall*) – the main verb never changes.

Unit 6 Future tenses

3 **Make the sentences negative.**

1 He will help me cook dinner.
   He won't help me cook dinner.
2 I'll help you with your homework.
   _____
3 You'll be very tired after playing tennis.
   _____
4 They will win the prize.
   _____
5 We'll give you a present.
   _____
6 I'll buy the red shirt.
   _____

4 **Write questions. Then answer the questions using the words in brackets.**

1 you / be / on holiday / in March
   (be at home)
   Will you be on holiday in March?
   No, I won't. I'll be at home.
2 we / arrive / at the hotel / in the morning
   (land in Spain)
   _____
   _____
3 you/ buy / the striped leggings
   (buy the plain leggings)
   _____
   _____
4 it / cost / a lot / to go to the show
   (be cheap)
   _____
   _____
5 the sun / shine / tomorrow
   (rain)
   _____
   _____
6 he / have / a career in music
   (become a famous actor)
   _____
   _____

be going to

Affirmative	Negative	Question
I am (I'm) going to work	I am not (I'm not) going to work	Am I going to work?
you are (you're) going to work	you are not (aren't) going to work	Are you going to work?
he is (he's) going to work	he is not (isn't) going to work	Is he going to work?
she is (she's) going to work	she is not (isn't) going to work	Is she going to work?
it is (it's) going to work	it is not (isn't) going to work	Is it going to work?
we are (we're) going to work	we are not (aren't) going to work	Are we going to work?
you (you're) going to work	you are not (aren't) going to work	Are you going to work?
they are (they're) going to work	they are not (aren't) going to work	Are they going to work?

Short answers

Yes, I am.   No, I'm not.
Yes, you are.   No, you aren't.
Yes, he/she/it is.   No, he/she/it isn't.
Yes, we/you/they are.   No, we/you/they aren't.

Future tenses **Unit 6**

We use *be going to* to talk about:

- plans and arrangements in the near future.
  We **are going to** try that new Italian restaurant tomorrow.
  He **is going to** take his driving test next week.

- something we know is going to happen because we have evidence.
  He's driving too fast. He**'s going to** crash!
  I didn't study. I**'m going to** fail the exam.

Notes

We can use either the present continuous (future meaning) or *be going to* for things we have arranged.
I**'m meeting** him on Saturday.
I**'m going to** meet him on Saturday.

5 Complete the sentences with the correct form of *be going to* and a verb from the box.

| ~~be~~ | clean | see | snow | study | travel |

1. I feel ill and I think I _____am going to be_____ sick!
2. We _____ a play at the theatre tomorrow evening.
3. He _____ his car later this afternoon.
4. The students _____ English at summer school.
5. We _____ to Australia for our holidays next month.
6. It's very cold. I think it _____ tonight.

6 Write what is going to happen.

1. I have got a swimsuit and a towel.
   I am going to go swimming.
2. He has got spaghetti, water and a saucepan.
   _____
3. I have eaten too much ice cream and I don't feel well.
   _____
4. Dad has got a brush, paint and a ladder.
   _____
5. They are tired and they are wearing pyjamas.
   _____
6. We are putting up decorations and making special food.
   _____

45

Unit 6 — Future tenses

7 Write questions.

1 It's going to rain before it gets dark.
   Is it going to rain before it gets dark?
2 You're doing the housework next week.
   _____
3 The teacher is meeting my parents next week.
   _____
4 We will be in trouble when the teacher arrives.
   _____
5 She's going to go to bed.
   _____
6 They're visiting the museum on Saturday morning.
   _____

8 Make the sentences negative.

1 They are going to pass their exams.
   They aren't going to pass their exams.
2 He is working tomorrow.
   _____
3 It will snow next July.
   _____
4 She's acting in the play this evening.
   _____
5 We're visiting the art galleries in Paris next week.
   _____
6 She'll be home before nine o'clock.
   _____

Time expressions with future tenses

in a minute	next year
in a while	this afternoon
later	this evening
next Monday	soon
next month	tomorrow
next week	tonight

He's going to finish **in a minute**.
I'm starting work **next Monday**.
We'll go and see her **tomorrow**.

9 Complete the sentences in your own words.

1 This weekend, I'm going to _____ go to the Natural History Museum _____ .
2 Soon my friend will _____ .
3 Next year, I'll _____ .
4 This evening, I'm going to _____ .
5 Tomorrow, I'm _____ .
6 Next summer, I'm _____ .

Unit 6 — Future tenses

10 Circle the correct answer.

1 'What would you like to drink?'
   'I ___ a milkshake, please.'
   a am going to have   b am having
   c will have

2 Look at that tree! It ___ fall down!
   a will   b is   c is going to

3 The plane ___ at nine o'clock this evening.
   a is going to leaving   b is leaving
   c will leaving

4 I ___ the bank manager the day after tomorrow.
   a am seeing   b going see
   c will seeing

5 She ___ sixteen next year.
   a will be   b is being   c is going

6 He ___ some new trainers at the weekend.
   a is going to buy   b buys
   c will buys

11 Find the mistakes in the sentences. Then write them correctly.

1 I promise <u>I'm being</u> home by eleven o'clock.
   <u>I promise I'll be home by eleven o'clock.</u>

2 He won't to help me do the gardening.
   _____

3 They're going learn English grammar.
   _____

4 Her friend will coming to visit later.
   _____

5 She is starting her new job next week?
   _____

6 My birthday party goes to be fantastic!
   _____

12 Find the extra word and write it in the space.

1 Will you <u>to</u> do the washing up? _____<u>to</u>_____
2 What are you going making for dinner? _____
3 Is he going to be drive all the way to Scotland? _____
4 He won't not come to my party. _____
5 They're be watching the match on TV on Saturday evening. _____
6 I'm going to go and shopping in the morning. _____

Pairwork

Work in pairs. Talk about your future. Think about the points below.

- your home
- your family
- your job
- your hobbies

Writing

Write a paragraph about what you think the world will be like one hundred years from now. Think about houses, education, pollution, cars, clothes and any other ideas of your own.

UNIT 7

Can, could and be able to

can

Affirmative	Negative	Question
I/you can play	I/you cannot (can't) play	Can I/you play?
he/she/it can play	he/she/it cannot (can't) play	Can he/she/it play?
we/you/they can play	we/you/they cannot (can't) play	Can we/you/they play?

Short answers	
Yes, I/you can.	No, I/you can't.
Yes, he/she/it can.	No, he/she/it can't.
Yes, we/you/they can.	No, we/you/they can't.

Can is a modal verb and is followed by the infinitive (without *to*).

We use *can*:

- to talk about ability in the present.
  He **can** speak Spanish.
  She **can** run fast.

- to ask for something (request).
  Can you pass me the salt, please?

- to talk about what is and isn't allowed in the present and in the future (permission).
  '**Can** I stay out late?' 'No, you **can't**.'

Notes

Can cannot be used in the future simple or in the present perfect simple.
We use *will be able to* or *have/has been able to* instead.

Can you speak Chinese, Grandpa?

I could when I was young, but I can't now.

Can, could and be able to Unit 7

1 Complete the sentences with *can* and the words from the box.

buy	explain	paint	play	post
	~~speak~~	stay	use	

Think about it!

Can always stays the same – you do not put -*s* with *he*, *she* and *it*.

1 He ___can speak___ Russian.
2 You _____ out until midnight tonight.
3 My brother _____ really good pictures.
4 _____ you _____ this letter for me, please?
5 The teacher _____ the grammar rules.
6 She is in the school orchestra because she _____ the flute very well.
7 _____ we _____ the computer this evening?
8 _____ I _____ some new trainers with the money you gave me?

2 Make the sentences negative.

1 They can understand Japanese.
   They can't understand Japanese.
2 A baby can drive a car.
   _____
3 Doctors can cure every disease in the world.
   _____
4 Plants can grow without water.
   _____
5 Astronauts can breathe without masks in space.
   _____
6 Computers can think like people.
   _____

3 Write sentences asking for permission.

1 stay out until after midnight
2 play my music loudly
3 order a pizza from the restaurant
4 book an adventure holiday
5 open the window
6 watch a film on my tablet

1 _Can I stay out until after midnight?_
2 _____
3 _____
4 _____
5 _____
6 _____

could

Affirmative	Negative	Question
I/you could play	I/you could not (couldn't) play	Could I/you play?
he/she/it could play	he/she/it could not (couldn't) play	Could he/she/it play?
we/you/they could play	we/you/they could not (couldn't) play	Could we/you/they play?

Short answers

Yes, I/you could.	No, I/you couldn't.
Yes, he/she/it could.	No, he/she/it couldn't.
Yes, we/you/they could.	No, we/you/they couldn't.

49

Unit 7   Can, could and be able to

> *Could* is a modal verb and is followed by the infinitive (without *to*).
>
> We use *could*:
>
> - to talk about past ability.
>   He **could** ride his bike very fast when he was a boy.
>
> - to ask for permission in the present or the future.
>   **Could** I use your pen for a minute?
>   **Could** I leave school early tomorrow?
>
> - to ask for something politely.
>   **Could** you take me home, please?

4   **Write *A* for ability, *P* for permission or *R* for request.**

1. Could he drive a car when he was twenty? _A_
2. Could you give me some extra help with my homework? ___
3. Could you buy me some toothpaste when you go out, please? ___
4. Could I stay at Mina's house tonight? ___
5. Could you speak English when you were four? ___
6. Could she swim fast a few years ago? ___
7. Could you drive me to the train station tomorrow, please? ___
8. Could we go out later if we finish our homework? ___

5   **Write polite requests using *could*.**

1. You are thirsty.
   Could I have a drink of water, please?

2. You haven't got a pen, but your friend has got two.
   _____

3. It is cold in your house and the window is open.
   _____

4. You need some money for your bus fare.
   _____

5. You have met an Italian teacher and you want to learn how to speak Italian.
   _____

6. You need help with your English homework.
   _____

Can, could and be able to — Unit 7

6 Write questions. Then answer the questions using the words in brackets.

1. he / ride / a motorbike / young (ride a bicycle)
   Could he ride a motorbike when he was young?
   No, he couldn't. He could ride a bicycle.

2. she / swim / a little girl (paddle in the sea)
   _____
   _____

3. they / cook spaghetti / young (help to make cakes)
   _____
   _____

4. your brother / rollerskate / ten years ago (ride a tricycle)
   _____
   _____

5. astronauts / fly to Saturn / in 1990 (walk on the moon)
   _____
   _____

be able to

Affirmative	Negative	Question
I am (I'm) able to visit	I am not (I'm not) able to visit	Am I able to visit?
you are (you're) able to visit	you are not (aren't) able to visit	Are you able to visit?
he is (he's) able to visit	he is not (isn't) able to visit	Is he able to visit?
she is (she's) able to visit	she is not (isn't) able to visit	Is she able to visit?
it is (it's) able to visit	it is not (isn't) able to visit	Is it able to visit?
we are (we're) able to visit	we are not (aren't) able to visit	Are we able to visit?
you are (you're) able to visit	you are not (aren't) able to visit	Are you able to visit?
they are (they're) able to visit	they are not (aren't) able to visit	Are they able to visit?

Short answers

Yes, I am.	No, I'm not.
Yes, you are.	No, you aren't.
Yes, he/she/it is.	No, he/she/it isn't.
Yes, we/you/they are.	No, we/you/they aren't.

We use *be able to* in most tenses.

Present simple: *I **am able to**, you **are able to**,* etc.
Past simple: *I **was able to**, you **were able to**,* etc.
Present perfect simple: *I **have been able to**, you **have been able to**,* etc.
Future simple: *I **will be able to**, you **will be able to**,* etc.

We use *be able to* to talk about ability in the past, present or future.
He **is able to** speak French.

Unit 7 Can, could and be able to

7 Rewrite the sentences using the past simple of be able to.

1 I could play the keyboard when I was younger.
   I was able to play the keyboard when I was younger.
2 Could your mother swim when she was a little girl?
   _____
3 I couldn't use the internet.
   _____
4 He could play the guitar very well.
   _____
5 She couldn't read English until she was six.
   _____
6 Could they always play football well?
   _____

8 Circle the correct answer.

1 (Could I) / Was I able to go to the US next year?
2 Can he / Has he been able to go to the cinema with his friends tonight?
3 Was I able to / Can I stay up late to watch TV this evening?
4 Could you / Will you able to help me to carry these bags, please?
5 I can / could lift heavy things now, but I couldn't when I was young.
6 She was able to / can go ice skating every weekend when she was a girl.

Can, could and *be able to* **Unit 7**

9 Complete the sentences with the words from the box.

> can   could   couldn't
> has been able to   were ... able to   ~~will be able to~~

1 Do you think astronauts _____will be able to_____ fly to all the planets one day?
2 I _____ dance well, but I'm not good at singing.
3 He _____ come to my party last Saturday because he wasn't very well.
4 She _____ speak four languages since she was six years old.
5 I can't speak German very well, but I _____ understand a lot when I was on holiday.
6 _____ you _____ eat nuts when you were young?

Pairwork

Work in pairs. Think of three things you want to do and ask your partner for permission to do them. Then tell your partner about three things you can do now which you couldn't do when you were younger.

Writing

1 Write a short paragraph about your abilities. Say what you can or can't do now and what you could or couldn't do ten years ago.

2 Write a short paragraph about what people in the 21st century can and can't do and what they could and couldn't do hundreds of years ago.

UNIT 8: Must/mustn't and have to/don't have to

must/mustn't

Affirmative	Negative	Question
I/you must visit	I/you must not (mustn't) visit	Must I/you visit?
he/she/it must visit	he/she/it must not (mustn't) visit	Must he/she/it visit?
we/you/they must visit	we/you/they must not (mustn't) visit	Must we/you/they visit?

Short answers	
Yes, I/you must.	No, I/you mustn't.
Yes, he/she/it must.	No, he/she/it mustn't.
Yes, we/you/they must.	No, we/you/they mustn't.

Must is a modal verb and is followed by the infinitive (without *to*).

We use *must*:

- to talk about obligation in the present or the future.
  You **must** wear a seatbelt in the car.

- to say that something is necessary in the present or in the future (necessity).
  I **must** go to the shops on the way home.

We use *mustn't*:

- to talk about prohibition in the present or in the future.
  You **mustn't** speak to your friends like that.

Notes
We cannot use *must* in the past simple. We use *had to* instead.

I must wear a helmet when I ride my bike.

Must/mustn't and *have to/don't have to* Unit 8

1 **Write *N* for necessity, *O* for obligation and *P* for prohibition.**
1 You must do your English homework every week. _O_
2 They mustn't eat in class. ___
3 You mustn't smoke in the doctor's waiting room. ___
4 I must study hard this year to pass the exams. ___
5 We mustn't make a noise because Dad's sleeping. ___
6 He must learn to drive before he can start his new job. ___
7 Must I do the washing up after lunch? ___
8 You must water the plants or they'll die. ___

2 **Write school rules.**

- eat food at your desk ✗
- keep your desk tidy ✔
- work hard ✔
- help each other ✔
- talk when somebody else is talking ✗
- be polite to everybody ✔
- listen to the teacher ✔
- go home early ✗

1 You mustn't eat food at your desk.
2 You must keep your desk tidy.
3 _____
4 _____
5 _____
6 _____
7 _____
8 _____

Think about it!

Must and *mustn't* always stay the same – you do not put *-s* with *he*, *she* and *it*.

have to/don't have to

Affirmative	Negative	Question
I/you have to visit	I/you do not (don't) have to visit	Do I/you have to visit?
he/she/it has to visit	he/she/it does not (doesn't) have to visit	Does he/she/it have to visit?
we/you/they have to visit	we/you/they do not (don't) have to visit	Do we/you/they have to visit?

Short answers		
Yes, I/you do.	No, I/you don't.	
Yes, he/she/it does.	No, he/she/it doesn't.	
Yes, we/you/they does.	No, we/you/they don't.	

Unit 8   Must/mustn't and have to/don't have to

Have to and *don't have to* are followed by the infinitive (without *to*).

We use *have to* in most tenses.

Present simple: *I* **have to**, *you* **have to**, etc.
Past simple: *I* **had to**, *you* **had to**, etc.
Present perfect simple: *I* **have had to**, *you* **have had to**, etc.
Future simple: *I* **will have to**, *you* **will have to**, etc.

We use *have to* to talk about obligation.
I **have to** *do a lot of work tonight.*

We use *don't have to* for things which are not necessary.
I **don't have to** *buy any bread. I bought some this morning.*

3 Write questions.

1 Do I have to tidy my room now?
   Yes, you have to tidy your room now.

2 _____
   Yes, you have to eat lunch before you watch TV.

3 _____
   No, they don't have to go home yet.

4 _____
   Yes, we have to do what the teacher says.

5 _____
   Yes, she has to stay at home this evening.

6 _____
   Yes, he has to pass his exams to go to university.

4 Write questions. Then answer the questions using the words in brackets.

1 I / cook / pasta / tonight (cook rice)
   Do I have to cook pasta tonight?
   No, you don't. You have to cook rice tonight.

2 the students / read poetry / today (write an essay)
   _____
   _____

3 you / buy / your own clothes (pay for my books)
   _____
   _____

4 we / get up early / on Saturdays (get up early on Mondays)
   _____
   _____

5 we / look after the baby / later (do our homework)
   _____
   _____

Must/mustn't and *have to/don't have to* **Unit 8**

5 **Complete the sentences with the correct form of *have to* or *don't have to* and the verbs from the box.**

> ~~cook~~   do   get up   help   make   wash

1 I don't _____have to cook_____ dinner tonight because we're going to eat out.
2 He _____ at seven o'clock every morning to go to school.
3 You _____ me – I can do it myself.
4 I will _____ a cake because it's Mum's birthday today.
5 Those clothes are very dirty. You'll _____ them now!
6 We _____ any homework tonight because tomorrow is a holiday.

6 **Match 1–6 with a–f. Then write sentences.**

1 It was hot yesterday.   a I have to study for my exams.
2 It's the summer holidays.   b I'll have to go to the doctor's later.
3 I feel ill.   c I don't have to water them again until tomorrow.
4 I can't come out with you this evening.   d I didn't have to wear a jacket.
5 I watered the plants this morning.   e I had to go to the dentist's this morning.
6 I had toothache last night.   f We don't have to go to school for weeks!

1 It was hot yesterday. I didn't have to wear a jacket.
2 _____
3 _____
4 _____
5 _____
6 _____

57

Unit 8 — Must/mustn't and have to/don't have to

must/have to and mustn't/don't have to

We often use *must* for internal obligation and *have to* for external obligation.
I **must** go to the gym. (I am very unfit.)
I **have to** make my bed. (My mother has told me to.)

We can use *must* and *have to* as if they had the same meaning.
I **must** go now.
I **have to** go now.

Mustn't and *don't have to* have very different meanings.
You **mustn't** touch the fire. It is dangerous.
You **don't have to** do your homework today. You can do it tomorrow.

7 Circle the correct answer.

1 I *don't have to* / *mustn't* go to work tomorrow because I'm on holiday.
2 The children *don't have to* / *mustn't* play football in the classroom.
3 He *mustn't* / *doesn't have to* make his lunch. His mum makes it for him.
4 You *don't have to* / *mustn't* forget to brush your teeth before you go to bed.
5 She *must* / *mustn't* ride her motorbike without a helmet.
6 I *have to* / *mustn't* tidy my bedroom this morning.

8 Find the mistakes in the sentences. Then write them correctly.

1 You <u>have wear</u> a hat when it's very cold.
   You have to wear a hat when it's very cold.

2 We don't must be rude to our teacher.
   _____

3 He has to does his homework before he can go out.
   _____

4 I have remember to lock the door when I go out.
   _____

5 Do you have to helped your father clean the car?
   _____

6 We mustn't using Mum's computer without her permission.
   _____

7 What time do they have to been home this evening?
   _____

8 I must to leave work early yesterday.
   _____

Must/mustn't and *have to/don't have to* — Unit 8

9 Find the extra word and write it in the space.

1 Does he have to had learn all the grammar by tomorrow? _____had_____
2 We mustn't to read magazines in the English lesson. _____
3 When I was young, I have had to walk to school. _____
4 He must to make three meals a day. _____
5 Doctors must be try hard to help all their patients. _____
6 Did you have to must eat all your dinner when you were young? _____

10 Complete the sentences in your own words.

1 It's snowing. I _____must wear my coat and boots_____ .
2 I'm tired. I _____ .
3 My English mark isn't very good.
   I _____ .
4 I haven't finished all my work.
   I _____ .
5 My room is untidy and Mum wants it to be tidy.
   I _____ .
6 I haven't got any money.
   I _____ .
7 Too much cola isn't good for you.
   I _____ .
8 It's very hot outside. I _____ .

Pairwork

Work in pairs. Tell your partner three things you are obliged to do – either at home, at school or at work. Then tell your partner three things you know you mustn't do when you are in a busy town.

Writing

1 Write a short paragraph about what students must and must not do if they want to get good exam results.

2 Write a list of the things you have to do and don't have to do next weekend.

Grammar review 2   Units 5–8

1 Complete the sentences with the past simple or the present perfect simple.

1 We _____left_____ (leave) the party at eleven o'clock.
2 Five years ago, we _____ (go) to Spain for our holidays.
3 She _____ (have) a baby since I last saw her.
4 What _____ (you / do) when you were in England?
5 What _____ (they / eat) last night?
6 They _____ (be) to four concerts already this year.
7 What _____ (you / eat) since you got up this morning?
8 We _____ (go) to the theatre last Saturday.

2 Complete the sentences with the words from the box.

| always | ~~for~~ | month | never | last | since | yesterday | yet |

1 We've been friends ____for____ years.
2 She has _____ seen an alligator.
3 He walked to the swimming pool _____ .
4 We went to the cinema at seven o'clock _____ night.
5 I lost my English book last week, but I've found it _____ then.
6 They've _____ wanted to see that band perform on stage.
7 Have they finished their homework _____ ?
8 I met my Australian cousin for the first time last _____ .

3 Circle the correct answer.

1 We ___ the house last week.
   a have sold   b were selling   (c) sold
2 Look! That boy ___ his arm.
   a broke   b has broken   c have broken
3 Have you ever ___ on a camel?
   a ride   b rode   c ridden
4 What ___ he say to the teacher yesterday?
   a has   b did   c was
5 ___ she worked in Africa?
   a Has   b Did   c Have
6 They've always ___ good students.
   a be   b were   c been
7 Did you ___ to the British Museum when you visited London?
   a went   b go   c gone
8 Have you ever ___ the colour of your hair?
   a changed   b change   c changes

4 Find the extra word and write it in the space.

1 We did went to the theatre last night. _____did_____
2 I have already made the beds and cleaned the kitchen now. _____
3 We've have just won a prize! _____
4 Where did they already get married? _____
5 He did built his house on the coast. _____
6 Where were you been an hour ago? _____

60

Units 5–8 **Grammar review 2**

5 Complete the sentences with the future simple or *be going to*.
1 I'm really hungry. I think I ___will order___ (order) a pizza.
2 I _____ (feed) your pets while you are on holiday in Portugal.
3 _____ you _____ (play) tennis tonight?
4 You _____ (not like) the film, so don't go and see it.
5 _____ I _____ (help) you with the housework?
6 We _____ (move) house tomorrow.
7 What _____ she _____ (buy) Dad for his birthday?
8 Be careful! You _____ (drop) the case on the floor.

6 Circle the correct answer.
1 Don't worry. You __ pass your exams.
   a are going to   b are   (c) will
2 __ I bring you something to drink?
   a Will   b Am   c Shall
3 Fatima is making dinner for everyone __ evening.
   a today   b this   c in
4 I __ meeting Annie at the café this evening.
   a going to   b am   c will
5 When __ the plane leaving?
   a is going to   b will   c is
6 He will be fourteen years old __ year.
   a next   b other   c soon
7 We are leaving the house __ a minute.
   a in   b on   c at
8 Bye, Daniel. I'll see you __ !
   a later   b next   c this day

7 Find the mistakes in the sentences. Then write them correctly.
1 She doesn't look very well. I think she <u>will</u> be sick.
   She doesn't look very well. I think she is going to be sick.
2 Is that heavy? I'm going to carry it for you.
   _____
3 I will have a party on Saturday.
   _____
4 Look at those dark clouds! It will rain.
   _____
5 Will we have lunch together tomorrow?
   _____
6 I promise I'm going to help you.
   _____
7 No, I don't know the answer. I'm going to phone Sarah and ask her.
   _____
8 Our flight will leaving at eight o'clock.
   _____

Grammar review 2 — Units 5–8

8 Circle the correct answer.

1 He *could* / *can* swim when he was two years old.
2 *Can* / *Am able* I have some money for a drink?
3 Tree frogs *could be* / *can* jump.
4 Will you *be able to* / *can* stay at my house on Saturday night?
5 Do you think he *could* / *will be able to* play football so well when he was young?
6 *Could* / *Able* you bring me a glass of water, please?
7 He isn't *can* / *able to* come to school today.
8 We *can't* / *not able to* wait any longer.
9 She *was* / *can't* able to walk before she was one.
10 *Am I able to* / *Can I* borrow your bike tomorrow?

9 Complete the sentences with *can*, *could*, *was* or *will*.

1 She _____was_____ not able to go to the party.
2 _____ you be able to come to the party next week?
3 _____ he read when he was three?
4 When _____ I go on holiday with my friends?
5 Look! _____ you see that man? I think he's a famous actor.
6 When _____ you be able to write back to me?
7 They _____ not wait to meet their friend at the airport.
8 I tried very hard, but I _____ not able to understand the lesson.
9 I don't think I _____ give you any money. I haven't got any!
10 _____ I leave class early tomorrow?

10 Find the extra word and write it in the space.

1 She couldn't to understand what he was saying. _____to_____
2 Could you to tell me where the supermarket is, please? _____
3 Are you be able to play tennis with me at the weekend? _____
4 I can't not hear very well with my right ear. _____
5 She couldn't done sing so well when she was a teenager. _____
6 Do you think they will can be able to come? _____
7 He is can play the guitar like a rock star. _____
8 Can he able finish his work in time? _____
9 The cat was able to could climb down from the tree. _____
10 The students who have finished their test can to leave. _____

Units 5–8 **Grammar review 2**

11 **Complete the sentences with *must, mustn't, has/have to* or *doesn't/don't have to*.**

1 Children _____mustn't_____ shout during lessons.
2 Does he _____ tidy his own room?
3 They _____ be polite to their parents.
4 Do you _____ wear a uniform at your school?
5 Mum _____ do the ironing because Dad does it.
6 You _____ be rude to your boss.
7 Do you _____ drive on the right in Italy?
8 Emma _____ do any homework because she is only three.
9 We _____ do this homework until next week.
10 She _____ get up at six o'clock every morning to go to work.

12 **Find the extra word and write it in the space.**

1 She must to leave the party early. _____to_____
2 We have to not get to school by half past eight tomorrow. _____
3 You must to make notes on what the teacher says. _____
4 What must I be do to show I'm sorry? _____
5 They don't have to must pay for the computer now. _____
6 Why does he do have to stay in tonight? _____
7 You mustn't be walk in the middle of the road. _____
8 Must I to do this exercise? _____

13 **Find the mistakes in the sentences. Then write them correctly.**

1 I <u>mustn't</u> finish my homework before tomorrow.
   I must finish my homework before
   tomorrow.

2 I'll must go to bed early tonight.
   _____
   _____

3 People not must waste water.
   _____
   _____

4 You have to go to the dentist's regularly?
   _____
   _____

5 What time do she have to start work tomorrow?
   _____
   _____

6 We mustn't driving too fast.
   _____
   _____

7 Do you have walk to school?
   _____
   _____

8 I don't having to get up early on Saturdays.
   _____
   _____

UNIT 9

Relative clauses

Relative clauses

Relative clauses give us more information about the person, animal or thing we are talking about. We use relative pronouns (*who*, *which*, *where*) to introduce this information. They come after the noun they refer to.

The girl is called Leena. She gave me this pen. → The girl **who** gave me this pen is called Leena.
I've lost the key. The key opens my suitcase. → I've lost the key **which** opens my suitcase.
That's the school. I had English lessons there. → That's the school **where** I had English lessons.

We use:

- **who** for people.
  He's the man **who** shouted at me.

- **which** for animals or things.
  This is the house **which** my parents have bought.

- **where** for places.
  That's the town **where** I grew up.

They won the match! She's the player who scored the goal, and that's the cup which they won.

Relative clauses Unit 9

1 Complete the sentences with *who, which* or *where*.
1. Dad is taking us to the village _____where_____ he was born.
2. Is this the page _____ we have to read for homework?
3. Is that the boy _____ stole your pen?
4. The car _____ is outside the house is my brother's.
5. The girl _____ won the race is called Molly.
6. I know a good restaurant _____ we could go this evening.
7. Where's the money _____ I left here?
8. Yesterday I met someone _____ went to the same school as me.

2 Circle the correct answer.
1. I don't read books __ are very long.
   a who   b where   (c) which
2. Is that the house __ you lived ten years ago?
   a which   b where   c what
3. Those are the students __ got the best marks in English.
   a who   b what   c which
4. Is that the café __ we're meeting later?
   a who   b where   c which
5. Is he the boy __ lives next door to you?
   a what   b where   c who
6. India is a country __ you can see elephants in the wild.
   a where   b who   c which
7. Have you see my bag __ has got my books in?
   a which   b where   c what
8. This is the girl __ lives on my street.
   a which   b who   c where

3 Write sentences.
1. Gavin is a boy. He crashed my dad's car.
   Gavin is the boy who crashed my dad's car.
2. The Palace is a hotel. I work there.
   _____
3. This is my new bag. I bought it yesterday.
   _____
4. Those are new students. They are studying maths.
   _____
5. That's a photographer. She takes amazing photos of wildlife.
   _____
6. That's a fast food restaurant. We go there for milkshakes every Saturday.
   _____

Unit 9 Relative clauses

4 Find the extra word and write it in the space.

1 Is he the boy <u>for</u> who your brother went on holiday with? _____<u>for</u>_____
2 She's a good cook who is always makes tasty meals. _____
3 Here is the present which I bought it for your birthday. _____
4 Have you visited the place where William Shakespeare was born there? _____
5 Is she the woman who was used to be a singer? _____
6 I couldn't find the shop where you can buy which cheap jeans. _____
7 Ken is the man who knows a lot about it English grammar. _____
8 The girl who she helped me is over there. _____

5 Match 1–6 with a–f. Then write sentences.

1 That old factory is
2 My brother is
3 That's the
4 She is the teacher
5 Those are the roses
6 Have you seen the island

a hospital where I was born.
b where that famous actor lives?
c which we planted last year.
d the person who rescued the cat from the river.
e where my dad worked years ago.
f who explained the grammar rules to us.

1 <u>That old factory is where my dad worked years ago.</u>
2 _____
3 _____
4 _____
5 _____
6 _____

> **Think about it!**
>
> The relative pronoun always comes immediately after the noun it refers to.

6 Write the words in the correct order.

1 eyes / has / he / boy / green / got / the / is / who
   <u>He is the boy who has got green eyes.</u>
2 you / is / where / the / lived / place / this / ?
   _____
3 Amy / golf / who / is / the / plays / girl
   _____
4 that / the car / is / you / saw / which / ?
   _____
5 the house / where / that's / Luis / lives
   _____
6 I / tall / a man / two metres / met / who / is
   _____

Relative clauses Unit 9

7 Find the mistakes in the sentences. Then write them correctly.

1 That man over there is the person which taught me to swim.
   That man over there is the person who taught me to swim.

2 The house what they have bought is near the beach.
   _____

3 The man who is singing he is my brother.
   _____

4 We met a person yesterday was very polite.
   _____

5 Can I see where the laptop which your mum bought you?
   _____

6 This is the park which I first played football.
   _____

8 Complete the sentences with *who, which* or *where* and the phrases from the box.

| comes from Italy   ~~fly to the moon~~   lay eggs   lots of people work |
| makes people laugh   we learn interesting things |

1 Astronauts are people _____ who fly to the moon _____.
2 Tortoises are animals _____.
3 School is the place _____.
4 Factories are places _____.
5 Pizza is a food _____.
6 A clown is a person _____.

9 Complete the sentences in your own words.

1 I know a man _____ who owns a Ferrari _____.
2 I don't know anybody who _____.
3 I like to read books which _____.
4 I like people who _____.
5 I went on holiday to a place where _____.

Pairwork

Work in pairs. Talk to your partner about two people you know, two places you have been and two books you have read. Remember to use relative clauses.

Writing

Write about your family. Say something about the people, the place where you live, your house, your pets and the things in your house. Use relative clauses.

UNIT 10
Nouns and articles

Plurals

Regular plurals

We usually make a noun plural by adding -s.
- cat → cats
- girl → girls

When a noun ends in -s, -ss, -sh, -ch, -x or -o, we add -es.
- bus → buses
- kiss → kisses
- brush → brushes
- watch → watches
- fox → foxes
- potato → potatoes

When a noun ends in a consonant and -y, we take off the -y and add -ies.
- baby → babies
- lady → ladies

When a noun ends in a vowel and -y, we add -s.
- boy → boys
- donkey → donkeys

When a noun ends in -f or -fe, we usually add -ves.
- leaf → leaves
- wife → wives

BUT

- giraffe → giraffes
- roof → roofs

Do we need any food for our picnic?

Yes, we need some cheese and a loaf of bread to make sandwiches, and a cucumber and three tomatoes to make a salad.

Nouns and articles — Unit 10

Irregular plurals

Some nouns are irregular and we make them plural in different ways.

child	→	children
fish	→	fish
foot	→	feet
man	→	men
mouse	→	mice
sheep	→	sheep
tooth	→	teeth

Notes

We do not use *a* or *an* before a plural noun.
This is a newspaper.
These are newspapers.

1 Write sentences.

1 The car is new.
   The cars are new.
2 The butterfly is on the leaf.
   _____
3 The mouse has got a long tail.
   _____
4 The watch is broken.
   _____
5 The baby is crying.
   _____
6 Put the ball in the box.
   _____

Countable and uncountable nouns

Countable nouns

Most nouns are countable nouns and we can make them plural.

bird	→	birds
sandwich	→	sandwiches
mouse	→	mice

Don't forget that we do not use *a* or *an* with plural nouns. We can use the word *some* with plural nouns in affirmative sentences. We can use the word *any* with plural nouns in negative sentences and questions.

She's got a book.	→	*She's got **some books**.*
He hasn't got a brother.	→	*He hasn't got **any brothers**.*
Did you bring a book to read?	→	*Did you bring **any books** to read?*

Uncountable nouns

Some nouns are uncountable nouns and do not have a plural form.

bread	lemonade
cheese	luggage
chocolate	meat
furniture	money
hair	water

69

Unit 10 Nouns and articles

We do not use *a* or *an* with uncountable nouns. We can use the word *some* in affirmative sentences. We can use the word *any* in negative sentences. We can use *some* or *any* in questions.

I want **some cheese**.
He's got **some bread** and **water**.
They haven't got **any money**.
Is there **any milk** in the fridge?

We can use the following words to talk about quantities of uncountable nouns.

bread	a loaf of bread	two loaves of bread
cola	a can of cola	two cans of cola
lemonade	a glass of lemonade	two glasses of lemonade
milk	a carton of milk	two cartons of milk
rice	a bowl of rice	two bowls of rice
soup	a tin of soup	two tins of soup
tea	a packet of tea	two packets of tea
water	a bottle of water	two bottles of water

2 Write *C* for countable nouns and *U* for uncountable nouns, and write the plural if there is one.

Noun	C or U	Plural
1 egg	C	eggs
2 sugar	U	–
3 meat		
4 sandwich		
5 bread		
6 honey		
7 cherry		
8 butter		
9 salt		
10 bottle		

Think about it!

Uncountable nouns always stay the same – you do not add *-s* to make them plural.

3 Complete the sentences with *some* or *any*.

1 Have you got _____any_____ chocolate?
2 I want _____ bread and butter, please.
3 There isn't _____ rice left.
4 We have got _____ eggs.
5 Would you like _____ coffee?
6 There isn't _____ sugar in the cupboard.
7 Have you got _____ cheese?
8 There are _____ biscuits on the table.

70

Nouns and articles Unit 10

Articles

The indefinite article: a/an

We use the indefinite article:

- with singular countable nouns.
  *I saw **a** lizard.*
  ***An** elephant has big ears.*

- when we are not talking about something specific.
  *I need **a** pen.* (any pen)
  *Have you got **a** coat?* (any coat)

- before an adjective which is before a countable noun.
  *That's **an** interesting book.*
  *He owns **a** black horse.*

- to talk about people's jobs.
  *She's **an** airline pilot.*

4 **Complete the sentences with *a*, *an* or –.**

1. They've got ____a____ new car.
2. Would you like _____ orange?
3. Don't forget to buy _____ milk.
4. I bought _____ new shirt yesterday.
5. I want to get _____ new phone.
6. She's got _____ lovely hair.

Articles

The definite article: *the*

We use the definite article:

- with singular and plural countable nouns and with uncountable nouns.
  ***The** window is broken.*
  ***The** windows are broken.*
  ***The** tea is cold.*

- when we are talking about something specific.
  ***The** flowers which you bought are on **the** table.*

- when we are talking about something which is unique.
  ***The** Acropolis is in Athens.*
  ***The** sun is shining brightly today.*

- before the superlative form of adjectives and adverbs.
  *She is **the** youngest student in the class.*
  *That's **the** fastest I've ever run!*

- with musical instruments.
  *I play **the** piano.*
  *Do you play **the** drums?*

- with the names of seas (***the** Mediterranean*), rivers (***the** River Seine*), oceans (***the** Pacific Ocean*), deserts (***the** Sahara Desert*), mountain ranges (***the** Alps*), groups of islands (***the** Galapagos Islands*), some countries (***the** United States of America*), hotels (***the** Hilton Hotel*), cinemas (***the** Lido Cinema*) and newspapers (***The** Times*).

Unit 10 — Nouns and articles

We do not use the definite article or the indefinite article with:

- plural nouns when we are talking in general.
  People enjoy having barbecues.

- people's names.
  I see Ruth every day.

- names of roads.
  They live in Bridge Street.

- names of towns and cities.
  He's going to London next week.

- names of individual mountains, lakes and islands.
  Have you ever been to Tenerife?

- names of countries or continents.
  We love Australia.

- names of meals.
  I have breakfast at eight o'clock.

- nouns which describe abstract things.
  Beauty is not as important as kindness.

- the words *home, work, school, hospital, prison* and *bed*, when we are talking in general.
  Did you know David was in hospital?

5 Complete the sentences with *the* or –.

1 My grandmother is in ____–____ hospital at the moment.
2 The Leaning Tower of Pisa is in _____ Italy.
3 Let's stay at _____ Ambassador Hotel when we're in London.
4 Do you like _____ animals?
5 Who is _____ oldest person you know?
6 What time are we having _____ lunch?
7 They liked _____ present which I bought them.
8 Have you seen _____ Jim?

6 Complete the sentences with *a*, *an*, *the* or –.

1 There is ____a____ swimming competition on Saturday.
2 I didn't know you were _____ nurse.
3 Look at _____ apples on that tree!
4 He's always wanted to visit _____ Greek islands.
5 Having _____ patience is a good quality.
6 She's _____ very intelligent person.
7 Do you go to _____ school on Mondays?
8 I would like _____ cup of tea, please.

7 Find the mistakes in the sentences. Then write them correctly.

1 He <u>is artist</u> and he paints brilliant pictures.
   He is an artist and he paints brilliant pictures.

2 Let's buy any bread and cheese and go for a picnic.
   _____

3 I love practising a piano every day.
   _____

4 It's great to swim in a sea.
   _____

5 There are two cartons of milks in the fridge.
   _____

72

Nouns and articles — Unit 10

8 Circle the correct answer.

1. Are you ___ man who repairs computers?
   a any   **b the**   c one
2. My father is ___ police officer in London.
   a the   b –   c a
3. Have you ever been to ___ Finland?
   a a   b –   c the
4. They're going on a cruise around ___ world.
   a a   b any   c the
5. Have you met ___ people who live next door?
   a –   b a   c the
6. There isn't ___ furniture in our new house yet.
   a some   b the   c any
7. Have we got ___ soap?
   a any   b an   c a
8. Where are ___ Rocky Mountains?
   a some   b the   c any

9 Complete the sentences with the words from the box.

> a   an   any (x2)
> some (x2)   the (x2)

1. The new Marvel film is on at _____the_____ Waterside Cinema.
2. Let's buy _____ chocolate for Samira.
3. Have you ever seen _____ Giza Pyramids?
4. He's _____ really rude person!
5. They haven't got _____ tea or coffee.
6. Do you want _____ apple juice?
7. I saw _____ elephant at the zoo.
8. Is there _____ milk in the fridge?

Pairwork

Work in pairs. Tell each other about an excursion or trip you have been on. Think about the points below.

- where you went
- what sights you saw
- what you ate and drank
- how you got there
- what you did there
- what time you got home

Writing

Write about a city you know well. Think about the points below.

- where it is
- what's special about it
- what sights there are
- what activities you can do there
- if there is a library, sports centre, theatre, etc.
- if you like it

UNIT 11 Quantifiers, *too* and *enough*

> We need a few eggs, a lot of flour and a little milk.

Quantifiers: *a little/a few/a lot of/lots of*

We use *a little* with uncountable nouns. It means *not much*.
There's **a little** cola left in the bottle.

We use *a few* with plural countable nouns. It means *some*. We can use *of* with *a few*.
There are **a few** children in the park.
A few of my friends went on holiday together.

We use *a lot of* with uncountable nouns and with plural countable nouns. It means *much/many*. We usually use it in an affirmative sentence. We can also use *lots of*, which has the same meaning.
We've got **a lot of/lots of** information to read.
There are **a lot of/lots of** students in my class.

1 Complete the sentences with *a few* or *a little*.

1 We only have _____a little_____ time before the guests arrive.
2 I'm going shopping. There are _____ things I need.
3 There are _____ eggs in the fridge.
4 He wants to put _____ salt and pepper on his dinner.
5 I knew _____ of the people at the party, but not many.
6 We saw _____ swans on the pond when we were in the park yesterday.
7 _____ of my friends are going to the cinema this evening.
8 I drank _____ water, but I wasn't very thirsty.

Quantifiers, *too* and *enough* **Unit 11**

2 Circle the correct answer.

1. I need __ sugar for this recipe.
   a a few   (b) lots of   c little of
2. I've got __ books about the environment at home.
   a a little   b a lot   c a few
3. There were __ people at the concert last night.
   a a little of   b a lot of   c few of
4. There is __ bread left.
   a a little   b a few   c a lot
5. Would you like __ strawberries with your ice cream?
   a a few   b a little   c lot of
6. We only need to add __ butter to the potatoes.
   a an   b a little   c a lot

3 Complete the sentences with *much* or *many*.

1. I haven't seen _____many_____ tourists so far this year.
2. He doesn't want _____ people to come to his party.
3. She doesn't want _____ salt on her food.
4. Do you know _____ students who are studying chemistry?
5. We don't have _____ money, but we're happy.
6. There isn't _____ time, so you must hurry.

both/either/neither

We use *both*, *neither* and *either* to talk about two people, animals or things. *Both* means one and the other. *Neither* means not one and not the other. *Either* means one or the other.

Both + plural affirmative verb
We can use *of* with *both*.
Both Sarah and Kate are my best friends.
Both of the girls live near me.

Neither + singular affirmative verb
We can use *of* with *neither*.
Neither Tim nor David has been abroad.
Neither of them has travelled by plane.

Either + plural or singular verb
We can use *of* with *either*.
Either John or Jim is going to collect you from work.
Do **either of** your brothers like lettuce?

Think about it!

You use *a little* for uncountable nouns and *a few* for countable nouns. You can use *a lot of/lots of* to talk about both countable and uncountable nouns.

Quantifiers: *much* and *many*

We use *much* with uncountable nouns in negative sentences and questions.
*There isn't **much** bread in the bag.*
*Is there **much** milk left?*

We use *many* with plural countable nouns.
We usually use it in negative sentences and questions.
*There aren't **many** young children in my family.*
*Are there **many** shops in your town?*

75

Unit 11 Quantifiers, *too* and *enough*

4 Complete the sentences with *both*, *either* or *neither*.

1 Can you believe that ____neither____ of those men helped to put the fire out?
2 The library hasn't got _____ of the books I want.
3 'Which colour T-shirt shall I buy?' '_____ the blue one or the black one.'
4 I love geography and history – _____ subjects interest me very much.
5 Could _____ of you help me carry this case upstairs?
6 _____ of the twins is good at maths.
7 I'm thinking of studying _____ art or English at university.
8 _____ Filip and Abi have piano lessons.
9 We can have _____ broccoli or courgettes with our dinner.
10 _____ of those hats suits you.

all/none

We use *all* and *none* to talk about more than two people, animals or things. *All* means every one of them. *None* means not even one of them.

All + plural affirmative verb
We can use *of* with *all*.
All the children do sport.
All of them are going to the party.

None + singular or plural affirmative verb
We always use *of* with *none*.
None of those boys does sport.
None of them are going to the party.

5 Circle the correct answer.

1 They are *neither* / (*both*) good at chess.
2 Are *all* / *either* the students in your group going on the trip?
3 We can have *both* / *either* soup or spaghetti for lunch.
4 *Neither* / *All* the computers have broken down.
5 *None* / *Both* of the books he lent me were very interesting, so I didn't read them.
6 *Either* / *Both* Mum or Dad will give you a lift to the station.

Quantifiers, *too* and *enough* Unit 11

too much/too many

We use *too much* and *too many* to talk about a quantity that is bigger than we want or need.

Too much + uncountable noun
There's **too much** salt in this soup.

Too many + plural countable noun
There are **too many** people on this bus!

6 Complete the sentences *much* or *many*.

1 Is there too ____much____ butter on the bread?
2 I think there are too _____ people on the train. It's not safe.
3 I don't want to do too _____ jobs today because I'm tired.
4 They wanted to take too _____ luggage on the plane.
5 I can't go out tonight. I have too _____ homework to do.
6 Do you think there are too _____ cars on the roads these days?

not enough

We use *not enough* to talk about a quantity that is smaller than what we want or need.

Not enough + uncountable noun or countable noun
There's **not enough** sugar in my coffee.
There are**n't enough** chairs for everyone.

7 Complete the sentences with *too much*, *too many* or *not enough*.

1 There are ___not enough___ chairs for everyone, so some people will have to stand.
2 I believe there's _____ litter on the streets. It's bad for the environment.
3 There are _____ things for young people to do in my town, so we get bored.
4 I've eaten _____ cakes and now I feel sick!
5 There is _____ time to watch the film tonight.
6 Don't give that little boy _____ chocolate to eat.
7 There are _____ factories in big cities, so the air is polluted.
8 There is _____ pizza for everyone. I'll buy more.

Unit 11 Quantifiers, *too* and *enough*

8 Circle the correct answer.

1 There were *too much* / *(a few)* people at the concert last Saturday.
2 We haven't got *enough* / *none* money to buy that laptop.
3 *None* / *Too many* of the students really understood the teacher's explanation.
4 I can't give you *not enough* / *a lot of* money because I haven't got much.
5 Washing the car is *too many* / *too much* trouble.
6 I need *none* / *a little* cheese for the top of the pizza.
7 Could you give me *too much* / *a little* rice, please?
8 There is *not enough* / *too much* coffee. Please can you make some more?

9 Find the mistakes in the sentences. Then write them correctly.

1 There is too many traffic in the city centre.
   There is too much traffic in the city centre.
2 I'm only taking a few luggage with me on holiday this year.
   _____
3 Neither of the people in my town recycle their bottles.
   _____
4 There are enough trees in the park. We must plant more.
   _____
5 Either of my parents understands computers.
   _____
6 There's too many noise coming from your room again!
   _____
7 Do you know none of the students at your university?
   _____
8 There are a little sandwiches and some fruit left for lunch.
   _____

10 Complete the sentences with the words from the box.

| both   either   lot of   much   neither   ~~not enough~~ |

1 There are __not enough__ teachers in our school. They need to employ more.
2 I don't eat a _____ fresh food, but I know it's good for you.
3 I think footballers earn too _____ money.
4 _____ my brothers passed their exams, so Dad took them out for ice cream to celebrate.
5 _____ of my parents has been to London.
6 We can go to _____ the cinema or the fast food restaurant – you choose!

Quantifiers, *too* and *enough* Unit 11

11 Match 1–6 with a–f. Then write sentences.

1 He can speak a lot   a all your money?
2 Have you spent   b homework to do?
3 Has he got much   c of languages.
4 There's not enough money   d studying languages?
5 Are they both   e milk left in the fridge.
6 There's only a little   f to buy all the shopping.

1 He can speak a lot of languages.
2 _____
3 _____
4 _____
5 _____
6 _____

12 Circle the correct answer.

1 There are too ___ things to carry.
   a much   b enough   **c many**
2 Can I have a ___ sugar for my coffee, please?
   a few   b little   c lot
3 ___ of my family enjoys watching sport on TV.
   a Either   b Both   c None
4 There is ___ time to do everything I want to.
   a too many   b not enough   c a few
5 I'm happy to go and see ___ of the films.
   a neither   b none   c either
6 I haven't done ___ housework this week.
   a many   b not enough   c much
7 ___ people care about the environment.
   a Too much   b Not enough   c None
8 I need ___ fruit for this recipe.
   a a lot of   b too many   c both

Pairwork

Work in pairs. Ask each other questions about what you usually eat.

Writing

Write a paragraph about the food young people eat. Give some advice on how young people could improve their diet.

UNIT 12 Past perfect simple

Past perfect simple

Affirmative	Negative	Question
I had (I'd) stopped	I had not (hadn't) stopped	Had I stopped?
you had (you'd) stopped	you had not (hadn't) stopped	Had you stopped?
he had (he'd) stopped	he had not (hadn't) stopped	Had he stopped?
she had (she'd) stopped	she had not (hadn't) stopped	Had she stopped?
it had (it'd) stopped	it had not (hadn't) stopped	Had it stopped?
we had (we'd) stopped	we had not (hadn't) stopped	Had we stopped?
you had (you'd) stopped	you had not (hadn't) stopped	Had you stopped?
they had (they'd) stopped	they had not (hadn't) stopped	Had they stopped?

Short answers

Yes, I/you had.   No, I/you hadn't.
Yes, he/she/it had.   No, he/she/it hadn't.
Yes, we/you/they had.   No, we/you/they hadn't.

He had learnt to swim before he went kayaking.

Past perfect simple — Unit 12

The past perfect simple is formed with *had* and the past participle of the main verb.

We use the past perfect simple to talk about:

- something that happened in the past before another action in the past. For the action that happened first we use the past perfect simple, and we use the past simple for the other action.
  *After I **had been** to the bakery, I **went** to the chemist's.*
  *Before he **watched** TV, he **had done** his homework.*

- something that happened before a specific time in the past.
  *He **had had** his meeting by three o'clock.*

1 Write *PS* if the verb is in the past simple and *PPS* if the verb is in the past perfect simple.

1 He went to school and studied hard. _____PS_____
2 She had studied a lot for the test. _____
3 We watched the football last Saturday and our team won. _____
4 They came to the party and danced all night. _____
5 By 1970, men had walked on the moon. _____
6 Had he eaten all those sandwiches by twelve o'clock? _____
7 She had a shower this morning. _____
8 By the end of the afternoon he had read five books. _____

2 Write questions.

1 She had washed her hair before the party.
   Had she washed her hair before the party?
2 He had fallen asleep by two o'clock.
   _____
3 Dad had got up before the sun rose this morning.
   _____
4 She had eaten too much.
   _____
5 The artist had painted twenty pictures by 2016.
   _____
6 They had tidied their room by lunchtime.
   _____

Unit 12 Past perfect simple

3 Complete the sentences with the past perfect simple.

1 They __had finished__ (finish) their dinner before Mum got home.
2 I _____ (do) my homework before I watched the film.
3 Everybody _____ (go) home by midnight.
4 They _____ (have) breakfast by the time Dad woke up.
5 She _____ (make) some great food for the party.
6 They _____ (decide) what to buy before they went shopping.

4 Complete the sentences with the past participle of the verbs from the box.

| ask | do | go | pass | send | start | ~~stay~~ | think |

1 He was tired because he had ____stayed____ up late the night before.
2 I called to see you yesterday, but you had _____ out.
3 I phoned Reena to invite her to the party, but you had _____ her already.
4 Mum asked me to do the ironing for her, but I'd already _____ it.
5 I'd _____ you a text message by the time you emailed me.
6 I suggested going to the Italian restaurant, but Gill had already _____ of it.
7 She was happy because she had _____ all her exams.
8 We were late and the film had _____ by the time we reached the cinema.

Time expressions

after
before
by (a time or date)
by the time

After she had done the ironing, she sat down and had a coffee.
Before he bought a new TV, he had checked the prices in lots of different shops.
By 1st May, I had moved house.
By the time I arrived, the film had finished.

Past perfect simple Unit 12

5 Write sentences with *after*. Use the words in brackets.

1 When did he eat his dinner? (watch TV)
    He ate his dinner after he had watched TV.

2 When did the sun start shining? (the rain stop)
    _____

3 When did he buy those trainers? (save enough money)
    _____

4 When did you make that cake? (read the recipe)
    _____

5 When did they get their marks? (teacher return from his holiday)
    _____

6 When did your brother pass his test? (have twenty driving lessons)
    _____

6 Write sentences with *before*.

1 finish the book / fall asleep
    I had finished the book before I fell asleep.

2 make lunch / do the ironing
    _____

3 charge my tablet / go online
    _____

4 study the grammar tables / do my English homework
    _____

5 have a shower / brush my teeth
    _____

6 get dressed / have my breakfast
    _____

7 Circle the correct answer.

1 We *tidy* / *(had tidied)* the living room before Mum came home from work.
2 We always *have* / *had had* our lunch before we watch TV.
3 *Had* / *Did* he eaten all the biscuits?
4 The film *hadn't finished* / *didn't finish* by the time we left the cinema.
5 The children *felt* / *had felt* ill because they had eaten too much ice cream.
6 Tom had learnt to ski before he *had gone* / *went* to Austria.
7 The children *had been* / *were* happy because it had snowed all night.
8 After we *had slept* / *sleep* for an hour, we felt much better.

Unit 12 Past perfect simple

8 Rewrite the sentences with *had* in the correct place.

1 The team was disappointed because they lost the match.
   The team was disappointed because they had lost the match.

2 We finished our exam by ten o'clock.

3 They been abroad twice before they went to England.

4 We always wanted to see the Statue of Liberty.

5 He wasn't hungry because he eaten a huge lunch.

6 They stayed up late, so they were tired in the morning.

9 Complete the sentences with the past simple or the past perfect simple.

1 He _____was_____ (be) very thirsty because he __hadn't had__ (not have) a drink all day.

2 The teacher _____ (say) he was disappointed because she _____ (not do) her homework.

3 She _____ (not travel) to many countries before she _____ (become) a famous singer.

4 The prisoner _____ (escape) by the time the police officers _____ (arrive).

5 They _____ (sell) all the nice jeans before I _____ (get) to the shop.

6 He _____ (not look) at many cars before he _____ (decide) this was the one he wanted.

Think about it!

When there are two actions in the past, always think about which action happened first. That is the action we put into the past perfect.

84

Past perfect simple Unit 12

10 Find the mistakes in the sentences. Then write them correctly.

1 Dad had left home before I <u>had</u> got up this morning.
  Dad had left home before I got up this morning.

2 She eaten all the nuts and didn't leave any for me!

3 Have you been to Africa before your dad took you last year?

4 I read the book by the time the lesson started.

5 We didn't see a real lion before we went to the zoo.

6 I didn't know it had rained until I had gone outside.

11 Write sentences.

1 My brother went out at seven o'clock. I got home at half past seven.
  My brother had gone out before I got home.

2 I drank a glass of milk at five o'clock. I felt sick at quarter past five.

3 The burglar stole our TV. The police arrived an hour later.

4 She put sunglasses on. Then she went outside for a walk.

5 He went to bed at eleven o'clock. It started snowing at midnight.

6 Mum charged her mobile phone. Then she sent a text message.

Unit 12 — Past perfect simple

12 Tick (✓) the correct sentence, a or b.

1 a Had the students have a good time on the field trip? ___
   b Had the students had a good time on the field trip? ✓
2 a The teacher had explained it to us before we did the test. ___
   b The teacher had explained it to us before we had done the test. ___
3 a Pete had bought the tickets before I had arrived. ___
   b Pete had bought the tickets before I arrived. ___
4 a Mum was angry because we had made a mess. ___
   b Mum had been angry because we had made a mess. ___
5 a Giorgio already seen the film, so he didn't come with us. ___
   b Giorgio had already seen the film, so he didn't come with us. ___
6 a By the time the rain had stopped, we were all very wet. ___
   b By the time the rain has stopped, we are all very wet. ___

13 Match 1–6 with a–f. Then write sentences.

1 We had been asleep
2 I had put sun cream on
3 By the time I arrived,
4 I had downloaded the app
5 They had finished their homework
6 I had played tennis before

a by the time I arrived at their house.
b I had a shower.
c all my friends had left.
d before the alarm clock went off.
e a week before my tablet broke.
f before I went to the beach.

1 We had been asleep before the alarm clock went off.
2 _____
3 _____
4 _____
5 _____
6 _____

Past perfect simple — Unit 12

14 Complete the sentences in your own words. Use the past perfect simple.
1. By nine o'clock this morning _____I had eaten breakfast_____ .
2. Before I arrived at school today, _____ .
3. Before I went to bed last night, _____ .
4. My friend was sad because _____ .
5. We all felt cold because _____ .
6. After I had done my homework yesterday, _____ .

Pairwork

Work in pairs. Tell each other about two things you had done, two places you had visited and two games you had played before you were six years old.

Writing

Read the list of times and events, and write a paragraph explaining what happened at Mr and Mrs Worth's house last Saturday night. Use the past perfect simple and time expressions.

6:30 p.m. – Mr and Mrs Worth lock the front door of their house
6:35 p.m. – Mr and Mrs Worth get into their car and drive to the theatre
7:00 p.m. – it gets dark
8:30 p.m. – a big lorry drives up to the house and two men get out
8:35 p.m. – the two men check that there are no lights on in the house
8:37 p.m. – they break a window and climb in
8:40 p.m. – the thieves check the whole house to see what is valuable
9:00 p.m. – the thieves take the TV and computer from the living room
9:15 p.m. – they put the stolen things into the lorry
9:20 p.m. – they drive away from the house
10:30 p.m. – Mr and Mrs Worth return home and find out about the burglary
10:40 p.m. – Mrs Worth rings the police
11:00 p.m. – the thieves escape along the motorway
11:15 p.m. – the police set up road blocks to catch the thieves

Last Saturday night, Mr and Mrs Worth decided to go to the theatre. Before they got into their car and drove to the theatre, they had locked the front door of their house …

Grammar review 3 — Units 9–12

1 Complete the sentences with *who* or *which*.

1 This is the photograph ___which___ he showed me.
2 He's the man _____ helped me with my luggage.
3 I like the book _____ you lent me last week.
4 That's the road _____ leads to our school.
5 Are you the person _____ knows all about sports?
6 English is the only subject _____ I can do really well.
7 Is this the boy _____ knows your brother?
8 I went to London on a train _____ was very dirty.

2 Complete the sentences with *which* or *where*.

1 Where is the pen ___which___ I was using?
2 That's the factory _____ John works.
3 He lives in a town _____ there are no trees.
4 Is this the bag _____ you lost last night?
5 Is that the shop _____ you left it?
6 Isn't that the hospital _____ you were born?
7 Have you seen a film _____ is about teenage pop stars?
8 This is the place _____ it happened.

3 Find the extra word and write it in the space.

1 This is the girl who I was telling you about her. ___her___
2 Do you know who the restaurant where we're going tonight? _____
3 Is Ahmed the person who knows all about which cooking? _____
4 Have you been to a which place where they sell furniture? _____
5 Where are the children who they are going to sing to us? _____
6 This isn't the meal which we who ordered! _____
7 Do you know a shop where I can buy which nice trainers? _____
8 Look! There's a place where there we can have a picnic. _____

4 Circle the correct answer.

1 Where are the earrings ___ your grandmother gave you last week?
   (a) which   b who   c what
2 There's a great restaurant in town ___ you can buy cheap pizzas.
   a which   b where   c who
3 The woman with the big hat is the one ___ lives on our street.
   a which   b what   c who
4 Is that the cottage ___ you used to live?
   a which   b where   c what
5 I don't know the actor ___ is starring in this film.
   a who   b which   c who he
6 That's the film ___ I told you about yesterday.
   a what   b which   c who

88

Units 9–12 Grammar review 3

5 Complete the sentences with the plural form of the noun in brackets.

1 They sell fantastic _____toys_____ (toy) in that shop.
2 We waited ages and then three _____ (bus) came along at the same time.
3 You can't buy those shoes. Your _____ (foot) are too big!
4 She used a lot of _____ (potato) to make these chips.
5 We must be quiet because the _____ (baby) are asleep.
6 Are you scared of _____ (mouse)?
7 Let's put all the shoes back in the _____ (box).
8 Put the _____ (brush) away when you have finished your painting.
9 There were a lot of _____ (child) at the baseball match.
10 She went to the dentist's and had two of her _____ (tooth) taken out.

6 Look at the underlined nouns and write C for countable noun and U for uncountable noun.

1 There were two kittens in the garden. C
2 Let's have a cheese sandwich for lunch. ___
3 Is there any milk in the fridge? ___
4 My grandfather grows his own tomatoes. ___
5 You often eat rice with Indian food. ___
6 How do bees make honey? ___
7 I'm going to fill my bottle with water. ___
8 Can I have the strawberry off the top of your ice cream? ___

7 Complete the sentences with some or any.

1 Would you like _____some_____ orange juice?
2 There's _____ milk in the carton.
3 I don't want _____ butter on my bread, thanks.
4 They bought _____ new furniture last weekend.
5 Are there _____ cherries in the bowl?
6 I don't want _____ chocolate – I'm on a diet.
7 You can't take _____ luggage with you in the helicopter.
8 Do you want _____ coffee?

8 Complete the sentences with a, an, the or –.

1 Where is _____the_____ cake I bought?
2 I didn't know your brother was _____ driving instructor.
3 You mustn't look straight at _____ sun.
4 Have you ever seen _____ elephants drinking?
5 That was _____ interesting documentary we watched last night.
6 What time shall we have _____ lunch?
7 I'm so glad I live in _____ France!
8 Have you ever skied in _____ Alps?

89

Grammar review 3   Units 9–12

9 Circle the correct answer.

1. We've only got *(a little)* / *a lot of* money left.
2. Do you eat *a lot of* / *a few* sugar every day?
3. There's only *a lot of* / *a little* cheese left, so don't use it all.
4. There are *a few* / *a little* eggs in the bird's nest.
5. *A few of* / *A little of* my friends are coming round to my house tonight.
6. There aren't *a few of* / *a lot of* biscuits left.
7. I left *a few* / *a little* things at your house.
8. I only want *lots of* / *a little* milk in my coffee, please.

10 Complete the sentences with *much* or *many*.

1. You haven't eaten _____much_____ food.
2. Have you visited _____ foreign countries?
3. How _____ furniture will they need when they move house?
4. How _____ times have I told you not to do that?
5. There aren't _____ people I know who can speak Japanese.
6. Do you know if there is _____ salt in this soup?
7. We must hurry! There isn't _____ time.
8. I'm pleased to see there isn't _____ pollution on this beach.

11 Complete the sentences with the words from the box.

| all   both (x2)   either (x2)   neither |
| none (x2) |

1. _____Both_____ history and geography are interesting subjects.
2. I don't like _____ of these books very much.
3. I've asked all my friends, but _____ of them want to come with me.
4. _____ Greg or Emilia will help you to wash the car.
5. _____ Frank and Otto will help you to clean the house.
6. I've eaten all the chocolate – there's _____ left.
7. _____ of the two girls understands the question.
8. _____ of those people live on my street. They are my neighbours.

12 Complete the sentences with *too much*, *too many* or *not enough*.

1. There were __not enough__ people at the party. It was very quiet.
2. Do you think young people spend _____ time on the internet?
3. There are _____ chairs for all the guests to sit on. I'll get some more.
4. You have put _____ salt in the spaghetti. It tastes horrible!
5. You can't finish your homework if there is _____ time.
6. I've got _____ bags. I can't carry them all!
7. 'Shall we make some ice cream?' 'No, there's _____ milk.'
8. There were _____ people in the queue for tickets, so we went home again.

Units 9–12 **Grammar review 3**

13 Complete the sentences with the past perfect simple.
1 I _had travelled_ (travel) to England before I could speak English.
2 They _____ (know) each other for five years before they got married.
3 She _____ (see) the play before in London.
4 He felt tired because he _____ (stay) up very late the night before.
5 I was surprised to see that it _____ (snow) during the night
6 She _____ (not think) about it very carefully before she decided.
7 _____ (they / hear) of malaria before they went travelling?
8 Where _____ (you / live) before you moved to Barcelona?

14 Complete the sentences with the past simple or the past perfect simple.
1 She _had made_ (make) dinner by the time I ____got____ (get) there.
2 He _____ (be) sick because he _____ (eat) too much chocolate cake.
3 We _____ (see) a lot of flats before we _____ (choose) this one.
4 I _____ (not go) to the concert because they _____ (sell) all the tickets.
5 He _____ (pass) his exams after he _____ (take) them three times!
6 By the time I _____ (get) to the cinema, the film _____ (start).
7 _____ (she / have) a shower before she _____ (go) to work this morning?
8 I _____ (finish) my homework before Dad _____ (get) home.

15 Circle the correct answer.
1 I called to see you, but you had ___ out.
   a go   (b) gone   c went
2 He ___ very excited because he had won the lottery.
   a had been   b had being   c was
3 We couldn't go out until after the rain ___ .
   a has stopped b stops   c had stopped
4 I saw the film ___ I had read the book.
   a then   b after   c by
5 I knew someone ___ in my garden.
   a had been   b has been   c have been
6 The beach ___ dirty because there had been a storm.
   a is   b had been   c was
7 ___ I got to school, the lesson had finished.
   a By the time b After   c By six o'clock
8 I had drunk lots of water before I ___ for a run.
   a had been   b go   c went

91

UNIT 13 Questions and *so/neither*

Question tags

He is an actor, isn't he?
You speak German, don't you?
They are doing their homework, aren't they?
You will tell her, won't you?
He's going to win the race, isn't he?
You paid for the milkshakes, didn't you?
She has forgotten the keys, hasn't she?
They had left already, hadn't they?
You can come to the party, can't you?
Let's go to the cinema, shall we?

He isn't very clever, is he?
He doesn't like tennis, does he?
We aren't leaving already, are we?
We won't be late, will we?
You're not going to pay me, are you?
She didn't stay till the end, did she?
I haven't upset you, have I?
You had never been there before, had you?
He can't help out tonight, can he?
Let's not argue, shall we?

We make questions tags with an auxiliary verb and a pronoun.
David likes tennis, **doesn't he?**

When the sentence is affirmative, we use a negative question tag.
He is right, **isn't he?**

When the sentence is negative, we use an affirmative question tag.
Parveen isn't ready, **is she?**

The question tag for *I am* is *aren't I?*
I'm late, **aren't I?**

We don't have to go to school today, do we?

No, we don't. Let's go to the park, shall we?

Unit 13 — Questions and so/neither

> We use question tags:
> - to confirm our opinion.
>   *This party is great, **isn't it**?*
> - when we are sure about what we are saying.
>   *You're Mary's daughter, **aren't you**?*

1 Complete the sentences with *is*, *isn't*, *are* or *aren't*.

1 You aren't angry, ___are___ you?
2 She is very tall, _____ she?
3 I am so silly, _____ I?
4 We _____ going to miss the film, aren't we?
5 He _____ joking, isn't he?
6 You _____ paying attention, are you?

2 Match 1–6 with a–f. Then write questions.

1 You forgot,   a doesn't she?
2 They didn't come,   b won't you?
3 She hasn't read the article,   c did they?
4 You will tell me the truth,   d didn't you?
5 He won't help me,   e has she?
6 She likes reading,   f will he?

1 You forgot, didn't you?
2 _____
3 _____
4 _____
5 _____
6 _____

Unit 13 Questions and so/neither

3 Complete the questions.

1 __He wasn't__ listening to the teacher, was he?
2 _____ going to buy a new car, aren't they?
3 _____ to the same school as my mum, didn't you?
4 _____ afford a new laptop, can we?
5 _____ played well this season, have they?
6 _____ starting to learn English, isn't he?
7 _____ like playing baseball, does he?
8 _____ watch TV very often, do they?

4 Complete the questions with a question tag from the box.

aren't we	can we	did they	did we
didn't they	hasn't he	~~is she~~	isn't she

1 She isn't enjoying the film, __is she__ ?
2 We're having pasta for dinner tonight, _____ ?
3 She's living in Barcelona at the moment, _____ ?
4 We didn't try hard enough, _____ ?
5 They didn't learn any German while they were on holiday, _____ ?
6 We can't wait much longer, _____ ?
7 They went to Greece on holiday, _____ ?
8 He has been to Australia and New Zealand, _____ ?

Think about it!

If the first part of the sentence is negative, the question tag will be affirmative. If the first part of the sentence is affirmative, the question tag will be negative.

5 Write the question tags.

1 India is in Asia, __isn't it__ ?
2 He failed his exams, _____ ?
3 They're going to town tomorrow, _____ ?
4 London is the capital of England, _____ ?
5 Kangaroos live in Australia, _____ ?
6 I told you that already, _____ ?
7 There aren't any penguins in Iceland, _____ ?
8 She can speak English really well, _____ ?

Questions and so/neither — Unit 13

Question words

We use questions words when we want more information than *yes* or *no*.

- *How*

We use *how* to ask about the way someone does something or to ask about someone's health.
How does he drive a car? (very carefully)
How is she? (She's much better now, thanks.)

We can use *how* with adjectives and adverbs.
How old are you? (thirteen)
How fast can he run? (very fast)
How quickly can you get here? (in five minutes)

- *Who*

We use *who* to ask about people.
Who is going to the theatre with you? (Sandra)
Who is that woman? (my grandmother)

- *What*

We use *what* to ask about things or actions.
What are you carrying? (my school books)
What does she do on Saturdays? (She plays volleyball.)

- *When*

We use *when* to ask about time.
When did you go to Asia? (in 2017)
When will he be ready? (soon)

- *Where*

We use *where* to ask about place.
Where have you been? (to the park)
Where did you buy that coat? (in Paris)

- *Which*

We use *which* to ask about one person or thing within a group of similar people or things.
Which girl is your sister? (the one with the long hair)
Which T-shirt will you buy? (the red one)

- *Whose*

We use *whose* to ask who something belongs to.
Whose car is this? (Miguel's)
Whose birthday is it today? (mine)

- *Why*

We use *why* to ask about the reason for something.
Why didn't he come to the cinema? (because he was working)
Why are they here? (because they want to speak to you)

6 Circle the correct answer.

1 Who / (How) did you travel to India?
2 Who / Whose house are you going to stay in?
3 Why / When don't you study harder?
4 What / Which are you going to study at university?
5 When / Which university are you going to go to?
6 Where / When is she leaving?
7 What / How do you usually do in the summer holidays?
8 When / Where were you when I phoned you?

7 Complete the questions with the words from the box.

how	~~what~~	when	where	which	who
		whose	why		

1 ___What___ did you do last night?
2 _____ aren't you coming to my party?
3 _____ is she feeling now?
4 _____ pair of shoes did you decide to buy?
5 _____ did you go on Saturday?
6 _____ car is that – William's or Mike's?
7 _____ do you think the party will finish?
8 _____ is going to play tennis with me tomorrow?

Unit 13 — Questions and *so/neither*

8 Circle the correct answer.

1 ___ did they do when they stayed at their grandparents' house?
   a When   b Where   **(c) What**

2 ___ book are you going to read first?
   a Who   b Which   c Why

3 ___ cut your hair?
   a Who   b Where   c When

4 ___ car are you going in?
   a Who   b When   c Whose

5 ___ aren't you coming to the park with us?
   a When   b Why   c Where

6 ___ have you put my umbrella?
   a Where   b Why   c When

7 ___ was the name of the film we saw last night?
   a When   b Where   c What

8 ___ did you break your leg?
   a Whose   b How   c Which

Subject/Object questions

Subject questions	Object questions
When we are asking about the subject of a sentence, the word order does not change. *Who made lunch?* (Mum made lunch.) *Which bag is the biggest?* (The red bag is the biggest.)	When we ask about the object of a sentence, the word order does change. *Who does he want to help?* (He wants to help his sister.) *What did he find on the beach?* (He found a bracelet on the beach.)

9 Write *SQ* for subject question and *OQ* for object question.

1 Who stole the car? **SQ**
2 Whose car did they steal? ____
3 Where did you go with your friend? ____
4 Who gave Mum a book for her birthday? ____
5 How many pizzas shall we order? ____
6 Which song do you want to listen to? ____
7 What have you bought today? ____
8 Who took him to the cinema? ____

10 Write questions.

1 Where _____ **did your Mum take you?** _____
   My mum took me to the café.
2 Where _____
   They bought their new clothes at the market.
3 Why _____
   I had a party because it was my birthday.
4 Who _____
   Sally plays chess really well.
5 What _____
   The burglar stole some money and the TV.
6 Whose _____
   It's Norman's car.

Questions and so/neither — Unit 13

so/neither

Tense	so	neither
Present simple: to be	She's lazy. So am I.	He isn't happy. Neither is she.
Present simple	I like rock music. So do I.	I don't live in this town. Neither do we.
Present continuous	I'm studying French. So is he.	Freya isn't watching TV. Neither am I.
Present perfect simple	Jasmin has gone to bed. So have the children.	I haven't seen him. Neither has she.
Future simple	We will go at the weekend. So will we.	I won't help you. Neither will I.
Past simple	Tom came to the party, So did Li.	We didn't bring a present. Neither did we.
Past perfect simple	She had left. So had he.	They hadn't forgotten. Neither had we.
Can (modals)	I can swim. So can I.	She can't speak English. Neither can he.

When we want to agree with an affirmative sentence, we use *so* + auxiliary verb + subject.
She has gone to London.
So has he.

When the main sentence doesn't have an auxiliary verb, we use *do*, *does* or *did* accordingly.
I like classical music.
So **do** I./So **does** Jim.

When we want to agree with a negative sentence, we use *neither* + auxiliary verb + subject.
I don't like sweetcorn.
Neither does she.

Notes

When the main verb in a sentence is *to be*, we use *so*/*neither* + *to be* + subject.

11 Complete the sentences with *so* or *neither*.

1 We aren't very happy.
    _____Neither_____ are we.

2 I can ride a horse.
    _____ can I.

3 We don't live in that neighbourhood.
    _____ do we.

4 She hasn't brought her homework.
    _____ has John.

5 I'm tired.
    _____ am I.

Unit 13 — Questions and so/neither

12 Complete the sentences.

1. I love watching athletics.
   _____So_____ do I.
2. We can't come to the party.
   _____ can we.
3. She doesn't want to leave.
   _____ does he.
4. They missed the bus.
   _____ I.
5. You haven't finished your lunch.
   _____ Ali.
6. Mary wants a new bike.
   _____ Karl.

13 Find the mistakes in the sentences. Then write them correctly.

1. <u>When</u> is he going on Saturday?
   <u>Where is he going on Saturday?</u>
2. Let's go out for a bike ride, don't we?
   _____
3. Who jacket is this?
   _____
4. 'They don't like it here.' 'Neither we do.'
   _____
5. Which colour is your new coat?
   _____
6. He's the English teacher, doesn't he?
   _____

14 Tick (✔) the correct sentence, a or b.

1. a Whose owns that red car outside? ___
   b Who owns that red car outside? ✔
2. a How times does he go fishing every week? ___
   b How many times does he go fishing every week? ___
3. a You aren't feeling sick, are you? ___
   b You aren't feeling sick, aren't you? ___
4. a When have you left your books? ___
   b Where have you left your books? ___
5. a Whose gave you this book about dinosaurs? ___
   b Who gave you this book about dinosaurs? ___
6. a Which of these films have you seen? ___
   b What of these films have you seen? ___

Questions and *so/neither* — Unit 13

15 Match 1–6 with a–f. Then write questions.

1 What   a   does the party start?
2 Who   b   are you going on holiday with?
3 How   c   are you going to wear to the party?
4 Whose   d   old is she?
5 Where   e   party is it?
6 When   f   does he live?

1 <u>What are you going to wear to the party?</u>
2 _____
3 _____
4 _____
5 _____
6 _____

16 Answer the questions in your own words. Write full sentences.

1 What is your favourite sport?
   <u>My favourite sport is sailing.</u>
2 Why are you studying English?
   _____
3 Where do you want to go for your next holiday?
   _____
4 How do you get to English lessons?
   _____
5 When do you do your homework?
   _____
6 Who is your favourite singer?
   _____

Pairwork

Work in pairs. Ask questions about your partner's family. Try to find out as much as you can.

Writing

Your friend has just moved to a new house in a different town one hundred kilometres away from you. Send him/her an email asking about his/her new home and the area it is in.

UNIT 14

Should/shouldn't and may/might

"I've got a cold."

"You should stay at home and drink lots of water. You shouldn't go outside until you are better."

should/shouldn't for advice

Affirmative	Negative	Question
I/you should listen	I/you shouldn't listen	Should I/you listen?
he/she/it should listen	He/she/it shouldn't listen	Should he/she/it listen?
we/you/they should listen	We/you/they shouldn't listen	Should we/you/they listen?

Short answers

Yes, I/you should.   No, I/you shouldn't.
Yes, he/she/it should.   No, he/she/it shouldn't.
Yes, we/you/they should. No, we/you/they shouldn't.

Should is a modal verb and is followed by the infinitive (without *to*).
We **shouldn't eat** so much chocolate.
You **should come** and see us more often.

We use *should*:

- to give advice.
  She **should** study harder.
  He **shouldn't** speak to her like that.

- to ask for advice.
  Should I buy a new laptop?

1 Write sentences. Use the words in brackets.

1 He's very tired. (go to bed / early)
   <u>He should go to bed early.</u>

2 They're thirsty. (drink / more water)
   _____

3 I feel sick! (not eat / lots of junk food)
   _____

4 I don't understand the lesson. (listen / to the teacher)
   _____

5 She can't cook. (read / recipe books)
   _____

6 They haven't got any money. (not buy / expensive trainers)
   _____

Should/shouldn't and *may/might* Unit 14

2 Write questions.

1 I / buy / the trainers / the boots
   Should I buy the trainers or the boots?
2 he / drive to work / walk to work
   _____
3 they / study / English / French
   _____
4 we / tidy / the living room / our bedrooms
   _____
5 I / go to university / get a job
   _____
6 they / drink / water / juice
   _____

may/might for possibility

Affirmative	Negative	Question
I/you may/might visit he/she/it may/might visit we/you/they may/might visit	I/you may not/might not visit He/she/it may not/might not visit We/you/they may not/might not visit	May/Might I/you visit? May/Might he/she/it visit? May/Might we/you/they visit?

We use *may* and *might* for possibility. They are modal verbs and are followed by the infinitive (without *to*).
It **may be** warm tomorrow.
Our grandparents **might visit** us on Saturday.

There is no short form for *may*. We must say *may not*.
He **may not** come with us.

There is a short form for *might* (*mightn't*), but we do not usually use it. We say *might not*.
She **might not** come with us.

3 Write answers with the words in brackets.

1 Where's Pete? (may / in the kitchen)
   He may be in the kitchen.
2 Why is the baby crying? (might / hungry)
   _____
3 Where are my keys? (may / on the table)
   _____
4 Who's at the door? (might / my friend Ahmed)
   _____
5 Where are my trainers? (may / in the cupboard)
   _____
6 How will they get here? (might / come by train)
   _____

4 Complete the sentences with *might not* or *should*.

1 Mum is tired. She ____should____ go to bed now.
2 The teacher is talking to us. We _____ listen to her and not talk in class.
3 We're going out now. We _____ be home until eleven o'clock.
4 If you're really sorry, you _____ tell her.
5 That computer _____ work because it's very old.
6 You _____ go to the dentist every six months.
7 We _____ always be polite to the teacher.
8 I _____ wear my jacket – it's very hot outside.

101

Unit 14 — Should/shouldn't and may/might

5 Circle the correct answer.

1 You ___ use the lift all the time if you want to get fit.
   a should   b might   (c) shouldn't

2 I ___ have enough money for both books, so I think I'll only buy one.
   a may   b might not   c shouldn't

3 We ___ go out in this weather without our hats. It's very cold!
   a should   b shouldn't   c might

4 I can hear a noise. I think there ___ be a cat in the garden.
   a should   b may not   c might

5 We ___ have lunch in the garden because it's a lovely day.
   a may   b shouldn't   c might not

6 The doctor says my leg ___ be broken.
   a should   b may   c shouldn't

6 Tick (✔) the correct sentence, a or b.

1 a We may to go to the fast food restaurant. ___
   b We may go to the fast food restaurant. ✔

2 a People should be drop litter on the streets. ___
   b People shouldn't drop litter on the streets. ___

3 a He may not want to have anything to eat yet. ___
   b He shouldn't not want to have anything to eat yet. ___

4 a You don't like water, so you should go snorkelling. ___
   b You don't like water, so you shouldn't go snorkelling. ___

5 a Do you think it should not be expensive to stay in that hotel? ___
   b Do you think it might be expensive to stay in that hotel? ___

6 a He shouldn't eat so many sweets! ___
   b He might not eat so too many sweets! ___

7 Rewrite the second sentence with a similar meaning to the first. Use the word in brackets.

Think about it!

Should, might and *may* are always followed by the infinitive (without *to*).

1 It's possible that Dad wants a cup of coffee now. (might)
Dad _____might want_____ a cup of coffee now.

2 It isn't a good idea to go to bed at twelve o'clock every night. (go)
You _____ to bed at twelve o'clock every night.

3 It's possible that Mum is in the bath at the moment. (may)
Mum _____ in the bath at the moment.

4 Do you think it's possible that he is at work today? (be)
Do you think he _____ at work today?

5 The doctor told Dad to take more exercise. (should)
The doctor said that Dad _____ more exercise.

6 It isn't a good idea to watch TV when you are doing your homework. (watch)
You _____ TV when you are doing your homework.

Should/shouldn't and *may/might* Unit 14

8 Complete the sentences in your own words.

1 What's your dad doing now?
   He might _____be making dinner_____ .
2 George doesn't get good marks in English.
   He should _____ .
3 There is a noise in the garden.
   It might _____ .
4 We want to drive to Portugal, but the car is old.
   The car might _____ .
5 The teacher isn't here.
   He may _____ .
6 Mum isn't at home now.
   She might _____ .

Pairwork

Work in pairs. Take turns to ask and answer. Think of three questions each.

Student A: Ask your partner for advice.

For example:

I want a new jacket, but I haven't got any money. What should I do?

Student B: Give your partner advice.

For example:

You should work on Saturdays to earn some extra money.

Writing

Your friend has just written to you for advice. He is going to travel round the world. Write an email including the points below.

- advice about what he should take, eat and wear
- what might happen to him on his journey

Hi _____ !

It was great to get your email. Your trip sounds very exciting! You asked me for some advice. Here it is!

I think you should _____ .

I don't think you should _____ .

On your journey you might _____
_____ .

I hope you have a brilliant time. Don't forget to send me some photos!

Love from,

_____

103

UNIT 15 First and second conditionals

First conditional

The first conditional is formed as follows:

If + present simple (*if* clause), future simple (main clause)

If you **go** to bed early, you **will not be** tired in the morning.
If he **doesn't do** well at school, his parents **won't be** very pleased.

We use the first conditional to describe something which will probably happen in the present or in the future.

Notes

When the *if* clause is before the main clause, we use a comma.
*If you help me at the weekend**,** I'll take you out for a meal.*

When the *if* clause is after the main clause, we don't use a comma.
*I'll take you out for a meal **if** you help me at the weekend.*

If I plant these seeds and water them, they will grow.

First and second conditionals Unit 15

1 Complete the sentences with the present simple.

1 If your team _____plays_____ (play) well, they will win the cup.
2 We will go out now if you _____ (be) ready.
3 He will clean the car if it _____ (not rain).
4 If they _____ (not want) to go to the cinema, we will stay at home.
5 If I _____ (pass) all my exams, Dad will buy me a new computer!

2 Complete the sentences with the future simple.

1 If the police officer catches the thief, she _____will put_____ (put) him in prison.
2 I _____ (help) you with your homework if you don't understand it.
3 If you don't iron your clothes, they _____ (not look) nice.
4 If she doesn't finish the work, they _____ (be) angry.
5 The children _____ (not get up) early if there is no school.

3 Write sentences in the first conditional.

1 you make lunch / I do the washing up
    If you make lunch, I'll do the washing up.
2 it snows / we go skiing
    _____
3 the restaurant is open / they have a meal there
    _____
4 you send me an email / I reply immediately
    _____
5 lose your new jacket / you be upset
    _____

4 Write answers using the words in brackets.

1 What will happen if the sun starts shining? (we go swimming)
    If the sun starts shining, we'll go swimming.
2 What will he do if he fails his English exam? (take it again)
    _____
3 What will you do if there is an earthquake? (hide under the table)
    _____
4 What will they do if their friend is ill? (phone a doctor)
    _____
5 What will we do if it rains tomorrow? (stay at home)
    _____

Unit 15 First and second conditionals

Second conditional

The second conditional is formed as follows:

If + past simple (*if* clause), *would* + infinitive (without *to*) (main clause)

If he **got** the job, he **would move** to London.
If she **was** very rich, she **would buy** a big house.

We use the second conditional:

- to talk about something which is impossible in the present or in the future.
  If you **were** a young child, you **would enjoy** that film.

- to talk about something which is possible in the present or the in the future but is unlikely to happen.
  If I **won** a lot of money, I **would be** very happy.

- to give advice. We usually use *were* instead of *was* the first and third person singular.
  If I **were** you, I would apologise to her.

Notes

The short form of *would* is *'d*. The short form can be used with all personal pronouns.
If I were you, I'd finish my homework.

---

5 **Complete the sentences using the words in brackets.**

1 If I won a prize (I give it to my mum)
   If I won a prize, I'd give it to my mum.

2 If there was a storm (she be frightened)
   _____
   _____

3 If she went to university (she study Italian)
   _____
   _____

4 If he were taller (he play basketball)
   _____
   _____

5 If we looked after the environment (the world be a more beautiful place)
   _____
   _____

6 If the teacher explained the grammar rules again (I understand them)
   _____
   _____

6 **Write answers using the words in brackets.**

1 What would you do if your tooth came out? (go to the dentist)
   If my tooth came out, I'd go to the dentist.

2 What would you do if you were late for class? (say sorry to the teacher)
   _____
   _____

3 What would you do if you won a holiday? (visit Australia)
   _____
   _____

4 What would you do if you broke your arm? (phone an ambulance)
   _____
   _____

5 What would you do if you lost your mobile phone? (look for it)
   _____
   _____

First and second conditionals Unit 15

7 Complete the sentences with the second conditional.

1. If I ____did____ (do) all the housework, my parents ____would be____ (be) very surprised.
2. My friend _____ (buy) lots of clothes if he _____ (have) more money.
3. If we _____ (eat) too much junk food, we _____ (get) stomach ache.
4. I _____ (help) you with your homework if I _____ (can).
5. If they _____ (think) it was a good idea, they _____ (sell) their house and move to the countryside.
6. I _____ (be) nervous if I _____ (have) an exam tomorrow.

Think about it!

Do not use *would* in the part of the sentence which includes *if*. Use the past simple.

8 Join the two sentences. Use the second conditional.

1. We live by the sea. We go swimming every day.
   If we didn't live by the sea, we wouldn't go swimming every day.
2. I eat fruit and vegetables every day. I'm very healthy.
   _____
3. I listen to the English teacher. I understand the grammar rules.
   _____
4. My friends are the same age as me. They are in my class.
   _____
5. Sally works hard. She passes all her exams.
   _____
6. He can speak good English. He has a job in London.
   _____

9 Write *1st* if the sentence or question is in the first conditional and *2nd* if it is in the second conditional.

1. If Martin phones, will you tell him that I am in the shower? __1st__
2. Will you clean the car if I wash the kitchen floor? _____
3. Would you like to live in the US if you had a lot of money? _____
4. I wouldn't be surprised if he failed the English exam. _____
5. If I were you, I wouldn't wear that purple T-shirt with those brown trousers. _____
6. If it isn't raining, we'll go for a long walk this afternoon. _____
7. You wouldn't like it if I told you the truth. _____
8. Will they go on a picnic tomorrow if it's sunny? _____

Unit 15 — First and second conditionals

10 Find the extra word and write it in the space.

1 What would you <u>have</u> do if you saw a big spider in the bath? _____have_____
2 If I will have enough money, I'll buy ice creams for everyone. _____
3 She won't be in the football team if she doesn't not train every day. _____
4 Will you be come to my party if I invite you? _____
5 If I went to Australia, would you do miss me? _____
6 If I were being you, I would buy the spotted shirt. _____
7 Will you cook dinner this evening if I would do the shopping? _____
8 Would you wear that coat if I will bought it for you? _____

11 Circle the correct answer.

1 I wouldn't drink that milk if I ___ you.
   a wasn't   (b) were   c am
2 If I'm tired, ___ go to bed at ten o'clock.
   a I'm   b I'd   c I'll
3 ___ you lend me some money if I promised to pay you back?
   a Would   b Will   c Were
4 Will you remind me to buy bread if I ___ ?
   a forgot   b forget   c forgotten
5 ___ buy a new bike if he had more money.
   a He will   b He had   c He would
6 If I were you, I ___ be nicer to my friends!
   a would   b will   c won't

12 Tick (✔) the sentence which means the same as the first sentence.

1 I would help you with your maths if I understood it better.
   a I won't help you because I don't understand maths well. ✔
   b I will help you because I understand maths better than you. ___
2 He would buy a new flat if he won the lottery.
   a He has got enough money for a new flat now. ___
   b He hasn't got enough money for a new flat now. ___
3 If she wasn't a nice person, she wouldn't have many friends.
   a She has got a lot of friends because she's nice. ___
   b She hasn't got a lot of friends because she isn't nice. ___
4 My parents would go skiing if they had more time.
   a My parents have got a lot of time to ski. ___
   b My parents haven't got a lot of time to ski. ___

First and second conditionals   Unit 15

13 Find the mistakes in the sentences. Then write them correctly.

1 If I don't sleep enough tonight, I <u>would</u> feel tired in the morning.
   <u>If I don't sleep enough tonight, I will feel tired in the morning.</u>

2 I'll lend you some money if you will need some.
   _____

3 I will watch TV all evening if there be some good programmes on.
   _____

4 I would feel ill if I eaten all that chocolate.
   _____

5 If it's windy tomorrow, we wouldn't go swimming in the sea.
   _____

14 Complete the sentences in your own words.

1 If I had a lot of money, <u>I would buy nice presents for all my friends</u>.
2 If it snows tomorrow, _____.
3 If I go to the shops on Saturday, _____.
4 If I study hard, _____.
5 If I passed all my exams, _____.

Pairwork

Work in pairs. Ask each other three questions beginning with *What will you do if …?*

For example:
What will you do if you fail your English exams?
What will you do if it snows during the night?

Use your imagination to make the questions fun!

Writing

Think of all the things you would like to do if you could, and think about what you would need to be able to do them.

For example:
- travel round the world (time and money)
- learn six foreign languages (to be very clever)
- buy a big house in Australia

Write a short article for your school magazine.

What I would do if I could!

If I had a lot of money, I would …

UNIT 16
Prepositions and reflexive pronouns

Let's tidy the kitchen. Put the plates and the cups on the shelves in the cupboards.

Prepositions of place

We use prepositions of place to talk about where something or someone is.

behind	in front of	on
between	near	opposite
in	next to	under

The hospital is **between** the park and the supermarket.
The fire station is **opposite** the bank.
The car is **in front of** the house.
Who do you sit **next to** at school?
I'll put your clothes **on** your bed.

We use *in* for countries and cities.
I live **in** England.
Do you live **in** Paris?

We use *at* for places that are smaller than a country or a city (*house, home, address, work, school*).
They are **at** the bank.
I live **at** 23, Old Bank Road.
Shall we meet **at** the park?
My sister is **at** work now.

1 **Complete the sentences with *in* or *on*.**

1 The books are _____on_____ the table.
2 The money is _____ my wallet.
3 The vase is _____ the TV.
4 Have you put your clothes _____ the wardrobe?
5 There are some vegetables _____ the fridge.
6 Let's hang the picture _____ the wall.
7 There is some jam _____ the cupboard.
8 Look at all those clouds _____ the sky!

110

Prepositions and reflexive pronouns Unit 16

2 **Circle the correct answer.**

1. I was born *in* / *opposite* Greece.
2. Your shoes are *under* / *between* the bed.
3. Do you sit *next to* / *on* Pablo in English lessons?
4. There is a police station *between* / *opposite* the supermarket.
5. He crashed the car because he didn't see the tree *under* / *in front of* him.
6. Is it far to the swimming pool, or are we *behind* / *near* it?
7. Are your brothers *at* / *on* school at the moment?
8. I can't see Yulia at the moment. She might be hiding *under* / *behind* a tree.

Prepositions of time

We use prepositions of time to talk about when something happens.

We use *in* for:

- months.
- years.
- centuries.
- seasons.
- periods of time.

We're getting married **in** June.
He died **in** 1999.
Did people have telephones **in** the 19th century?
We go on holiday **in** the summer.
I drink coffee **in** the mornings and tea **in** the afternoons.

We use *at* for:

- the exact time.
- points of time in a day.
- holidays and celebrations.
- the weekend.

The film starts **at** nine o'clock.
She has her lunch **at** midday.
We saw a parade **at** Notting Hill Carnival.
I don't go to school **at** the weekend.

We use *on* for:

- days of the week.
- dates.
- celebrations and holidays with the word *day* in them.

He does his shopping **on** Saturdays.
It's my birthday **on** 9th April.
We plant trees **on** Earth Day.

3 **Complete the sentences with *in*, *at* or *on*.**

1. He will be thirteen ____on____ 6th September.
2. I like going for walks _____ night.
3. What are you doing _____ Sunday?
4. I'll meet you outside the museum _____ the morning.
5. Do you go swimming _____ winter?
6. The party will finish _____ eleven o'clock.
7. Is your birthday _____ March or April?
8. What do you do _____ New Year's Day?

Unit 16 — Prepositions and reflexive pronouns

Prepositions of movement

We use prepositions of movement to express motion.

across	from	towards
along	through	up
down	to	

We cycled **along** the side of the road.
She fell **down** the stairs.
He kicked the ball **through** the window.
They walked **towards** the river and found a place for their picnic.

Reflexive pronouns

myself	himself	ourselves
yourself	herself	yourselves
	itself	themselves

We use reflexive pronouns:

- when the object and the subject of a sentence are the same.
  She enjoyed **herself** yesterday.
  He's talking to **himself**.

- with certain verbs (*behave, cut, enjoy, hurt*, etc.).
  Children, please behave **yourselves**!
  Ow! I've cut **myself** with the knife!
  Is he enjoying **himself**?
  Did you hurt **yourself**?

- with the verb *help* when it means take something (food or drink).
  Please help **yourselves** to more coffee.
  Can I help **myself** to a piece of cake?

- when we say that we did something without another person's help.
  I made this dress **myself**.
  Did he do his homework **himself**?

If we want to emphasise that we did something without help or to show that we did something alone, we can use the word *by* before the reflexive pronoun.

I leant to speak Japanese all **by myself**.
I went on holiday **by myself**.

4 Circle the correct answer.

1 Will you go *up* / *to* the chemist's for me when you go to town?
2 Why is he running *from* / *along* the street?
3 I don't like going *towards* / *up* ladders.
4 You must never walk *across* / *through* the road without looking.
5 The train is going *from* / *through* the tunnel.
6 What time are you coming home *to* / *from* school today?

5 Complete the sentences with the correct preposition.

1 Were there many people ____at____ the food festival?
2 What do you do _____ the evenings?
3 Who is that _____ the door?
4 I don't think you should swim _____ the river to the other side.
5 Where do you come _____ ?
6 Will you be here _____ eight o'clock in the morning?
7 The school is on the other side of the road, exactly _____ the park.
8 I'm not climbing _____ all those stairs!

6 Complete the sentences with the words from the box.

| I | ~~my brother~~ | they | you |
| | your mum | we | |

1 ____My brother____ travelled to New Zealand by himself.
2 Did _____ repair the car by herself?
3 _____ can't do all the housework by myself.
4 Are _____ going to enjoy themselves at the park?
5 _____ are organising the concert by ourselves.
6 Did _____ make all those cakes yourself?

Prepositions and reflexive pronouns Unit 16

7 Complete the sentences with the correct reflexive pronoun.

1 Did they enjoy __themselves__ at the concert?
2 Is she going to drive to Milan by _____ ?
3 Be careful! You might cut _____ !
4 I hate _____ for saying those terrible things to her.
5 Dad blamed _____ for crashing the car.
6 We hurt _____ playing football.

8 Circle the correct answer.

1 I don't think we can get that big table ___ the front door.
   a along   b down   (c) through
2 Will you be awake at six o'clock ___ the morning?
   a in   b on   c at
3 Can your sister make lunch by ___ ?
   a yourself   b herself   c yourselves
4 I'll be on holiday ___ August.
   a in   b to   c from
5 I'm late because I didn't know the lesson started ___ three o'clock today.
   a at   b to   c from
6 The baby boy walked by ___ for the first time yesterday!
   a herself   b himself   c itself

Think about it!

Reflexive pronouns always end in -self or -selves. Remember to match the reflexive pronoun to the subject of the sentence.

9 Find the mistakes in the questions. Then write them correctly.

1 Why don't you tidy your room **myself**?
   Why don't you tidy your room yourself?
2 Why don't we go skiing from December this year?
   _____
   _____
3 Is he doing all the decorating herself?
   _____
   _____
4 Who is that standing next on your mum?
   _____
   _____
5 Were you born on 2006?
   _____
   _____

Pairwork

Work in pairs. Talk about yourself and your family. What are the things you can do all by yourself? What are the things you prefer to do by yourself?

Writing

Write a description of your town, or a town you know, on a busy Saturday morning. Use as many different prepositions as you can.

Grammar review 4   Units 13–16

1 Write the question tags.

1 You're the English teacher, _aren't you_ ?
2 I'm good at playing tennis, _____ ?
3 He doesn't work very hard, _____ ?
4 They broke the computer, _____ ?
5 Let's buy a pizza, _____ ?
6 She can't ski, _____ ?
7 You drink a lot of milk, _____ ?
8 It's a good book, _____ ?

2 Write questions.

1 Where _____ did you see Peter _____ ?
   I saw Peter at the art gallery.
2 Which _____ ?
   I bought the yellow T-shirt.
3 How _____ ?
   He travels to school by bus.
4 Where _____ ?
   We spent the evening at Jamal's house.
5 Why _____ ?
   I shouted because I was angry.
6 When _____ ?
   I learnt to drive five years ago.
7 How _____ ?
   I'm fine, thanks.
8 Whose _____ ?
   It's Mary's car.

3 Match 1–6 with a–f. Then write questions and answers.

1 Who will make breakfast?
2 Who's going to play with him?
3 What has he bought a suit for?
4 Where did you see Martha?
5 What did he give her?
6 Who has made breakfast?

a Dad has.
b At the museum.
c Harry is.
d A birthday present.
e For his wedding.
f Jin will.

1 Who will make breakfast? Jin will.
2 _____
3 _____
4 _____
5 _____
6 _____

4 Complete the sentences.

1 I love eating ice cream.
   _So do_ I.
2 We can't go shopping this afternoon.
   _____ we.
3 She doesn't want to come.
   _____ he.
4 They forgot their keys.
   _____ I.
5 She didn't eat any of her food.
   _____ Jack.
6 You haven't done your work.
   _____ Aki.

Units 13–16 Grammar review 4

5 Rewrite the sentences with *should* or *shouldn't*.

1 We are rude to the teacher.
   We shouldn't be rude to the teacher.

2 He goes to bed late.
   _____

3 You don't eat enough vegetables.
   _____

4 People don't look after the environment.
   _____

5 She doesn't drink lots of water every day.
   _____

6 You eat so many biscuits!
   _____

6 Complete the sentences with *may*, *might not*, *should* or *shouldn't*.

1 It's snowing, so he ___might not___ drive over to see us today.
2 You _____ take more exercise if you want to get fit.
3 People _____ be cruel to animals.
4 It _____ be a good idea for Grandma to learn to ski.
5 You really _____ eat ice cream every day.
6 It _____ be difficult to pass the exam if you have revised.
7 There _____ be a lot of people at the cinema because it's a great film.
8 Don't wait for me – I _____ come.
9 We'll go out if we can, but it _____ rain.
10 I don't think you _____ spend so much money.

7 Circle the correct answer.

1 The phone's ringing – it ___ be Dad.
   (a) might   b shouldn't   c can
2 He ___ arrive late as there is a lot of traffic.
   a might not   b shouldn't   c may
3 The sun ___ shine today.
   a might   b shouldn't   c may to
4 Do you think it ___ snow?
   a shouldn't   b might   c might not
5 Everybody ___ learn something new from time to time.
   a shouldn't   b might not   c should
6 You ___ speak to people like that!
   a shouldn't   b should   c might not
7 Drivers ___ drive fast through city centres.
   a might not   b shouldn't   c should
8 We ___ work harder in English.
   a should   b might not   c shouldn't

115

Grammar review 4 Units 13–16

8 Complete the sentences with the first conditional.

1 If you say you're sorry, I __will forgive__ (forgive) you.
2 They'll get into trouble if they _____ (leave) school early.
3 If it rains this evening, we _____ (not go) to the park.
4 She won't be happy if you _____ (not tidy) your bedroom.
5 If I _____ (come) to the cinema, will you pay?
6 If people continue polluting the environment, what _____ (happen)?
7 Will you be disappointed if I _____ (not pass) my exams?
8 What will you study if you _____ (go) to university?

9 Complete the sentences with the second conditional.

1 If you ___left___ (leave) your keys on the bus, what would you do?
2 If the temperature _____ (fall) to five degrees, would you be happy?
3 What would you do if I _____ (give) you a lot of money?
4 Would you be ill if you _____ (eat) a kilo of bananas?
5 How would you go to work if there _____ (not be) any buses?
6 I would buy a new laptop if I _____ (have) more money.
7 If I met a film star, I _____ (be) excited.
8 Would your computer still work if you _____ (drop) it on the floor?

10 Circle the correct answer.

1 If I ___ the money, I would go on a cruise.
   a would had   b would have   (c) had
2 What ___ you do if you met your favourite singer?
   a if   b would   c did
3 I will cry ___ I watch a sad film.
   a would   b will   c if
4 If people don't stop hunting elephants, there ___ be any left soon.
   a will   b wouldn't   c won't
5 If he ___ drive, he would buy a Porsche.
   a could   b can   c would
6 I would ___ to New York if I had lots of money.
   a went   b go   c had gone
7 If you stop crying, I ___ buy you an ice cream.
   a would   b won't   c will
8 What will you ___ her if she asks you where you've been?
   a tell   b told   c will tell

Units 13–16 Grammar review 4

11 Circle the correct answer.
1. The bowl of fruit is *(on)* / *in* the table.
2. I'd like you to sit *at* / *between* Susan and me.
3. Sandra is *at* / *to* school today.
4. We live *near* / *under* the school.
5. If you look out of this window, you can see the park *next to* / *opposite*.
6. Let's meet *at* / *on* the bus station.
7. Don't walk right *near* / *in front of* me, or I'll step on your foot!
8. The salt is *next to* / *in* the pepper on the table.
9. My best friend lives *to* / *in* Barcelona.
10. I can't see you if you stand *between* / *behind* a tree!

12 Complete the sentences with *in*, *at* or *on*.
1. We moved here _____in_____ 2017.
2. Is your birthday _____ July or August?
3. She'll be home soon – she left the party _____ ten o'clock.
4. What are you doing _____ New Year's Day?
5. Did they eat traditional food _____ the festival?
6. The first exam is _____ 2nd June.
7. I'll see you _____ Monday.
8. I think I'll go horseriding _____ the weekend.
9. The show starts _____ seven o'clock.
10. Do you go skiing _____ winter?

13 Circle the correct answer.
1. I am taking the train *(to)* / *up* Liverpool.
2. All the children are walking *down* / *to* school.
3. Never walk *through* / *across* the road without looking both ways first.
4. It's not easy for her to walk *from* / *up* hills now that she has hurt her knee.
5. Jane is coming *down* / *along* the stairs with the baby in her arms.
6. We walked for miles *across* / *along* the path by the river.
7. He got lost coming home *from* / *to* the railway station.
8. All the cars were driving *across* / *towards* the coast on Friday evening.

14 Complete the sentences with the correct reflexive pronoun.
1. My sister fixed her bike by ____herself____ .
2. Is he going to the doctor's by _____ ?
3. We blamed _____ for causing the accident.
4. Don't cut _____ while you're preparing the vegetables.
5. They hurt _____ playing rugby.
6. Did she enjoy _____ at the party?

117

UNIT 17 Gerunds and infinitives

Gerunds

Gerunds are verbs with the *-ing* ending.
swimming
sleeping
playing

We can use the gerund:

- as a noun in a sentence.
  I like **swimming**.
  I love **sleeping**!
  I enjoy **playing**.

- as the subject of a sentence.
  Swimming is my favourite sport.
  Sleeping is my favourite hobby!
  Playing is something I enjoy.

- after prepositions.
  Don't leave without **saying** 'goodbye'.
  She's not very good at **playing** tennis.
  I'm interested in **learning** to drive.
  He's fed up with **helping** her to do her homework.

There are certain verbs and phrases which are followed by gerunds.

can't help
can't stand
dislike
(don't) mind
enjoy
hate
like
love
miss

She dislikes **waiting** for the bus in the rain.
I don't mind **looking** after the children tonight.
They can't stand **listening** to loud music.
In the winter, we miss **having** our meals in the garden.

Let's go climbing up that mountain. Climbing is my favourite sport.

OK! I like climbing too, and I want to take a photo at the top!

Gerunds and infinitives — Unit 17

1 Complete the sentences using gerunds.
1 He loves ____listening____ (listen) to the radio in the morning.
2 Do you mind _____ (look after) the baby while I go out?
3 The chocolates are delicious. I can't help _____ (eat) them.
4 Do you enjoy _____ (go) to the theatre?
5 The twins are afraid of _____ (walk) home in the dark.
6 I like _____ (drink) coffee in the morning.
7 She misses _____ (live) by the sea.
8 You can't stand _____ (do) the housework, can you?

2 Complete the sentences with the verbs from the box. Use gerunds.

| do | go | ~~learn~~ | play |
| study | swim | walk | work |

1 Do you like ____learning____ about English grammar?
2 I'm not very keen on _____ tennis.
3 I love _____ through the forest on a sunny day.
4 We don't like _____ the washing up.
5 He's very good at _____ a long way under water.
6 I'm interested in _____ engineering.
7 They enjoy _____ to the cinema.
8 She hates _____ in an office.

3 Tick (✓) the correct sentence, a or b.
1 a I can't help to cry when I watch a sad film. __
  b I can't help crying when I watch a sad film. ✔
2 a Jon hates going to the cinema without his friends. __
  b Jon hating going to the cinema without his friends. __
3 a They can't help to laughing at a funny joke. __
  b They can't help laughing a funny joke. __
4 a We enjoy wearing costumes at the festival. __
  b We enjoy wear costumes at the festival. __
5 a I mustn't go out without to tell Mum first. __
  b I mustn't go out without telling Mum first. __
6 a Sami is interested in learn Russian. __
  b Sami is interested in learning Russian. __

4 Write sentences.
1 smoke / be / bad for your health.
   Smoking is bad for your health.
2 dive / be / my favourite sport
   _____
3 do / maths / be / very difficult
   _____
4 water / the plants / keep / them alive
   _____
5 play / volleyball / be / great fun
   _____
6 study / hard / be / tiring
   _____

119

Unit 17 Gerunds and infinitives

Infinitives

Infinitives are verbs with the word *to*.
to walk
to watch
to read

We use the infinitive after certain verbs.

> afford
> allow
> ask
> decide
> hope
> offer
> persuade
> promise
> refuse
> want

He asked her **to help** him with his homework.
They offered **to lend** us their car.
I persuaded her **to come** with me.
She refused **to let** me pay for the meal.

We also use the infinitive after certain adjectives.

> amazed
> glad
> happy
> sad
> sorry
> surprised

She was sad **to leave** university.
I was surprised **to see** him at the party.

Notes
We can use the gerund or the infinitive after some verbs (e.g. *like, hate, love*) and the meaning stays the same.

I like **walking** in the rain.
I like **to walk** in the rain.

I like **studying** history.
I like **to study** history.

I love **travelling** by train.
I love **to travel** by train.

---

5 Complete the sentences with the verbs from the box. Use infinitives.

> buy   do   have   ~~help~~
> study   watch

1 He was very kind and offered ____to help____ me with my project.
2 The children are not allowed _____ TV after nine o'clock.
3 They decided _____ a party on Saturday night.
4 He persuaded me _____ a new pair of jeans.
5 Dad refused _____ any more work in the garden.
6 I want _____ in the UK.

6 Tick (✔) the correct sentences.

1 They have decided to buy a new car. ✔
2 Can you afford going to New Zealand on holiday? ___
3 I persuaded Dad to come to the fair with us. ___
4 I'm so glad to see you again. ___
5 I hope meeting you again soon. ___
6 They want to learn to drive. ___
7 I'm not allowed going to town on my own at night. ___
8 He refused lending me any money. ___

120

Unit 17 — Gerunds and infinitives

7 Complete the sentences with a gerund or an infinitive.

1 I don't mind ____working____ (work) hard.
2 We promise _____ (be) home by ten o'clock.
3 He enjoys _____ (go) to football matches.
4 They were surprised _____ (see) him.
5 I can't persuade her _____ (start) going to the gym.
6 Dad asked me _____ (buy) some bread from the bakery.
7 They miss _____ (eat) the lovely cakes their grandmother used to make.
8 We want _____ (get) good marks in the exam.

8 Complete the sentences with the words from the box.

| decided | hope | ~~learning~~ | telling |
| to leave | | | |

1 He enjoys ____learning____ about space travel.
2 Have you _____ to come with us to the museum?
3 Sarah was sad _____ her friends.
4 I _____ to travel a lot when I've saved up some money.
5 She doesn't believe in _____ lies!

9 Complete the sentences using the verbs in brackets.

1 I ____miss seeing____ (miss / see) our old neighbour.
2 She _____ (refuse / study), so she won't pass any of her exams.
3 Do you _____ (enjoy / stay) at home sometimes?
4 He has _____ (offer / take) me to the airport.
5 I _____ (not mind / come) with you to the doctor's.
6 Do you _____ (promise / work) harder next term?
7 He _____ (ask / play) in the team, but he wasn't good enough.
8 Jay _____ (persuade me / go) snowboarding last month.

10 Circle the correct answer.

1 Do you enjoy __ the only boy in your family?
   a to be   (b) being   c you are
2 He hates __ letters.
   a writing   b written   c to be writing
3 I persuaded Mum __ me a lift to town.
   a giving   b to gave   c to give
4 Do you mind __ me with all this work?
   a to help   b doing   c helping
5 They can't help __ sorry for the team that lost.
   a feeling   b to feel   c to be
6 I dislike __ horror films.
   a to watch   b to see   c watching
7 I'm sorry __ that you are leaving.
   a to hear   b hear   c hearing
8 Are you interested in __ to the match with me on Sunday?
   a coming   b to come   c will come

Think about it!

We use the gerund after verbs which describe what we like or don't like doing.

121

Unit 17 Gerunds and infinitives

11 Find the extra word and write it in the space.

1 We to enjoy studying English! ___to___
2 I'm interested in to finding out more about the history of Venice. _____
3 I hope to be get a job in London. _____
4 I like running, but I am hate going to the gym. _____
5 It can be dangerous the cycling on busy roads. _____
6 If I asked you nicely, would you to stop shouting? _____
7 I can't the persuade him to help me make lunch. _____
8 Do you want we to go to the beach on Sunday? _____

12 Find the mistakes in the sentences. Then write them correctly.

1 Swim is a great sport for keeping fit.
   Swimming is a great sport for keeping fit.
2 Have you decided to be going to France?
   _____
3 He doesn't mind plays games with his brother.
   _____
4 Did she offer helping you with the cooking?
   _____
5 Are you allowed stay out late on Saturdays?
   _____
6 I want writing a report about the environment.
   _____

13 Match 1–6 with a–f. Then write sentences.

1 He hates
2 We promise
3 I refuse to
4 The teacher doesn't mind
5 He asked
6 I love

a do that!
b going to the beach.
c to borrow some money.
d losing when he plays games.
e explaining the grammar rules to us again.
f not to do that again.

1 _He hates losing when he plays games._
2 _____
3 _____
4 _____
5 _____
6 _____

14 Rewrite the second sentence with a similar meaning to the first. Use the word in brackets.

1 I said I would tell the truth. (promised)
   I ___promised to tell___ the truth.
2 I hate to watch hospital programmes on TV. (stand)
   I _____ hospital programmes on TV.
3 'No, I'm not going to the dentist's,' said Henry. (refused)
   Henry _____ to the dentist's.
4 I don't want to eat any cake because I don't like it. (enjoy)
   I _____ cake.
5 'Can I borrow your bike?' asked Goran. (to)
   Goran _____ my bike.

122

Gerunds and infinitives Unit 17

15 Complete the sentences in your own words.
1 I can't afford _____to go on holiday this year_____ .
2 My mum persuaded me _____ .
3 I can't help _____ .
4 I love _____ .
5 I really hope _____ .
6 I really want _____ .

Pairwork

Tick (✔) what is true for you in the table below. Work in pairs. Tell your partner what you love, like, etc.

	love	like	dislike	can't stand
eat pizza				
watch horror films				
have music lessons				
swim in the sea				
go shopping				
surf the internet				
do housework				
go to the cinema				

Writing

Write an email to your new friend who lives in the UK. Tell him/her about yourself and what you like doing in your free time. Try to use gerunds and infinitives.

Dear _____ ,

Thank you for your email. It was interesting to read all about you. Now I'm going to tell you a bit about me!

I enjoy doing lots of different things. I love _____
_____ .

I really don't like _____

Sometimes at weekend I go out with my friends. We like _____
_____ .

Please write again soon.
Love, _____

UNIT 18 Passive voice

Passive voice: present simple affirmative

Present simple
The computer is used.
The computers are used.

The passive voice is formed with the verb *to be* and the past participle of the main verb.

Changing a sentence from active voice to passive voice happens as follows:

- The object of the active verb becomes the subject of the passive verb.
- We use the verb *to be* in the same tense as the verb in the active sentence.
- We use the past participle of the main verb in the active sentence.
- We use the word *by* if we want to say who or what did the action (the agent).

My mother makes dinner. → Dinner **is made by** my mother.
Dad cuts the grass. → The grass **is cut by** Dad.

We use the passive voice:

- to emphasise the action rather than the agent.
  My Dad **was attacked** yesterday.

- when we don't know the agent.
  Our car **was stolen** last night.

- when the agent is obvious.
  English **is spoken** in many countries. (by people)

My headphones were made in Germany and my phone was made in China.

Passive voice — Unit 18

1 Complete the sentences with *is* or *are*.

1 Dinner _____is_____ made by Dad.
2 The ironing _____ done by Mikhail.
3 The cats _____ chased by the dog.
4 The flowers _____ watered by the rain.
5 The newspaper _____ read by Mr and Mrs Wilson.
6 The windows _____ cleaned by the window cleaner.
7 A lot of rice _____ eaten in China.
8 The washing up _____ done by Anja.

2 Complete the sentences using the passive voice in the present simple.

1 Thieves __are caught__ (catch) by police officers.
2 Clothes _____ (make) by people called tailors.
3 Bread _____ (bake) by bakers.
4 Paintings _____ (paint) by artists.
5 Cars _____ (repair) by mechanics.
6 The *Mona Lisa* _____ (see) by thousands of people every year.
7 My hair _____ (cut) by a woman called Layla.
8 My eyes _____ (test) by the optician.

Passive voice: negatives and questions

The negative is formed by using the word *not* after the auxiliary verb.
Flowers are sold by florists. → *Flowers **are not sold** by bakers.*

The question is formed by putting the auxiliary verb in front of the subject.
Flowers are sold by florists. → ***Are** flowers **sold** by florists?*

3 Make the sentences negative. Then write answers using the words in brackets.

1 Yoghurt is made from cheese. (milk)
 Yoghurt isn't made from cheese.
 Yoghurt is made from milk.

2 Porsches are made in the UK. (Germany)
 _____
 _____

3 Honey is made by flies. (bees)
 _____
 _____

4 Tea is grown in Scotland. (India)
 _____
 _____

5 Thieves are put in hotels. (prisons)
 _____
 _____

6 Racing cars are driven by mechanics. (racing drivers)
 _____
 _____

Unit 18 Passive voice

4 Write questions.

1 fruit / sell / the butcher
   Is fruit sold by the butcher?
2 magazines / write / chemists
   _____
3 fires / stop / firefighters
   _____
4 cars / make / robots
   _____
5 football / play / astronauts
   _____
6 English / speak / at your school
   _____

Passive voice: past simple

Past simple

The computer was used.
The computers weren't used.
Were the computers used?

The past simple of the passive voice is formed in the same way as the present simple, but instead of using *am*, *is* or *are*, we use *was* or *were*.
The thief started the fire. → The fire **was started** by the thief.
Someone stole my keys yesterday. → My keys **were stolen** yesterday.

5 Complete the sentences with *was* or *were*.

1 My brother ___was___ hit in the eye by a tennis ball.
2 The window _____ broken by those boys.
3 The books _____ read by the children.
4 Who _____ the first plane made by?
5 The photographs _____ taken by my mum.
6 Our house _____ built a long time ago.
7 These chairs _____ made by my grandfather.
8 The race _____ won by Nikolaus.

6 Complete the sentences using the passive voice in the past simple.

1 The computer broke down and ___was fixed___ (fix) by a technician.
2 A lot of windows _____ (break) in last night's storm.
3 When I was a child, eggs _____ (bring) to us from the farm.
4 The present _____ (buy) by Harry.
5 At the party, all the food _____ (eat) by the guests.
6 *Romeo and Juliet* _____ (write) by William Shakespeare.
7 The carpets _____ (clean) by a specialist company.
8 The accident _____ (cause) by a bad driver.

Think about it!

If you want to be good at the passive voice, you need to know the past participle of the verb. Look up irregular past participles on page 164.

Passive voice Unit 18

7 Change the sentences from active to passive.

1 A boy on a bike hit my sister last week.
   My sister was hit by a boy on a bike last week.
2 Mark painted our house last month.
3 Dad bought a new laptop.
4 Someone stole my bag while I was shopping.
5 Mum made a cup of coffee.
6 A French chef prepared this meal.

8 Change the sentences from passive to active.

1 This table was made by my father.
   My father made this table.
2 This book was given to me by my best friend.
3 Her broken arm was X-rayed by the doctor.
4 Those flowers were given to the teacher by Billy.
5 Comic books aren't sold in that shop.
6 Thousands of burgers are made by fast food restaurants every day.

9 Write sentences. Use the words in brackets.

1 The science museum was opened by my mum. (the mayor)
   The science museum wasn't opened by my mum. It was opened by the mayor.
2 History is taught in zoos. (schools)
3 Cars are made in shops. (factories)
4 Planes are flown by bus drivers. (pilots)
5 The telephone was invented by Robert Ring. (Alexander Graham Bell)
6 The *Mona Lisa* was painted by a decorator. (Leonardo da Vinci)

10 Circle the correct answer.

1 Pasta __ eaten in Italy.
   a be   (b) is   c does
2 This car __ made in France.
   a are   b was   c has
3 Were your jeans __ from the market?
   a buy   b buyed c bought
4 __ your hair cut by a hairdresser?
   a Were b Was   c Did
5 Who was the thief caught __ ?
   a from b for   c by
6 The flowers __ delivered by the florist.
   a were b was   c been

127

Unit 18 Passive voice

11 Complete the sentences with the past participle of the verbs from the box.

build   compose   design   discover   invent   ~~make~~   watch   write

1 My shoes are _____made_____ of leather.
2 America was _____ by Christopher Columbus.
3 The Acropolis was _____ by the ancient Greeks.
4 *Swan Lake* was _____ by Tchaikovsky.
5 Radios were _____ by Marconi.
6 *Macbeth* was _____ by Shakespeare.
7 The dress was _____ by Stella McCartney.
8 The film was _____ by a lot of people.

12 Match 1–6 with a–f. Then write sentences.

1 The birthday cake   a was marked by the teacher.
2 Our bicycles   b was broken by a football.
3 My essay   c was made by my mother.
4 The race   d was won by Stefan.
5 The window   e was built ten years ago.
6 This house   f were repaired by the man in the shop.

1 The birthday cake was made by my mother.
2 _____
3 _____
4 _____
5 _____
6 _____

13 Tick (✓) the correct sentence, *a* or *b*.

1 a Were you taken to your hotel on the tour guide? ___
  b Were you taken to your hotel by the tour guide? ✓
2 a Was breakfast served in the dining room? ___
  b Were breakfast served in the dining room? ___
3 a Were the sun beds putted on the beach for you? ___
  b Were the sun beds put on the beach for you? ___
4 a Were the towels washed in a machine? ___
  b Were the towels washing in a machine? ___
5 a Were the ice creams be made in the hotel? ___
  b Were the ice creams made in the hotel? ___
6 a Were your room cleaned every day? ___
  b Was your room cleaned every day? ___

Passive voice — Unit 18

14 Find the mistakes in the sentences. Then write them correctly.

1 The football match <u>were</u> watched by thousands of people.
   The football match was watched by thousands of people.

2 The first goal was score by the captain.

3 The injured player was taken to hospital with ambulance.

4 My ticket to the match were bought by my best friend.

5 The players is wearing their blue T-shirts today.

6 The ball was stop by the goalkeeper.

15 Answer the questions in your own words.

1 Who is the ironing done by in your house?
   The ironing is done by my dad in my house.

2 Who were you fed by when you were a baby?

3 Who were you first taught English by?

4 Who was your bedroom decorated by?

5 Who was your hair cut by?

6 Who is your dinner made by?

Pairwork

Work in pairs. Take turns to ask and answer questions using the passive voice. Talk about the things that were done for you when you were a baby and young child.

- Who fed you?
- Who bathed you?
- Who read you stories?
- Who bought your clothes?
- Who took you out?
- Who taught you to read?

For example:
Who made your breakfast?   My breakfast was made by my mum.

Writing

Imagine you had a dream that you were taken to a strange land. Write about the points below and use the passive voice.

- How you were taken there.
- What happened while you were there.
- What were you given to eat and drink?
- What language was spoken?

Last night, I had a dream that I was taken to a very strange land! ...

UNIT 19
Comparatives, superlatives and adverbs of manner

Comparatives

We use the comparative to compare two people, animals or things.
*She's **older** than her brother.*
*Our car is **faster** than yours.*

We make the comparative form of most adjectives by adding *-er* to the adjective.
strong → stronger

When the adjective ends in *-e*, we add *-r*.
nice → nicer

When the adjective has one syllable and ends in vowel-consonant, we double the final consonant and add *-er*.
hot → hotter

When the adjective ends in *-y*, we take off the *-y* and add *-ier*.
easy → easier

We use the word *more* with some adjectives that have two syllables and the adjectives that have three or more syllables.
beautiful → more beautiful

Notes
We often use the word *than* after the comparative form.
*Rock climbing is **more dangerous than** golf.*

She's fitter than me. That's why she can run fast. I run slowly.

Comparatives, superlatives and adverbs of manner   Unit 19

1 Write the comparative form of the adjectives.

1 cold   _____colder_____
2 long   _____
3 funny   _____
4 lazy   _____
5 dangerous   _____
6 important   _____
7 tidy   _____
8 fat   _____
9 young   _____
10 nervous   _____

2 Complete the sentences with the comparative form of the adjective in brackets.

1 This butterfly is _____prettier_____ (pretty) than the one I saw yesterday.
2 Beth is _____ (clever) than Bob.
3 This exercise _____ (difficult) than the last one.
4 Our car is _____ (fast) than the bus.
5 My bedroom is _____ (tidy) than my brother's.
6 Geography is _____ (interesting) than history.
7 Your hair is _____ (long) than mine.
8 My sister is _____ (tall) than my brother.

Superlatives

We use the superlative form to compare more than two people, animals or things.
She's the **tallest** girl in the class.
Our house is the **oldest** of them all.

We make the superlative form of most adjectives by adding -est to the adjective.
strong → the strongest

When the adjective ends in -e, we add -st.
nice → the nicest

When the adjective has one syllable and ends in vowel-consonant, we double the final consonant and add -est.
hot → the hottest

When the adjective ends in -y, we take of the -y and add -iest.
easy → the easiest

We use the word *most* with some adjectives that have two syllables and the adjectives that have three or more syllables.
Who is the **most famous** actor in the world?

Notes
We use the word *the* before the adjective in its superlative form. We often use a phrase beginning with *in* or *of* to continue the sentence.

Unit 19 Comparatives, superlatives and adverbs of manner

3 Write the superlative form of the adjectives.

1 long — the longest
2 nice — _____
3 nasty — _____
4 fat — _____
5 beautiful — _____
6 quiet — _____
7 careful — _____
8 clean — _____

> **Irregular adjectives**
>
> Some adjectives are irregular and do not follow these rules.
> good → better → the best
> bad → worse → the worst
> much/many → more → the most
> little → less → the least
> far → further → the furthest

5 Complete the sentences with the comparative or superlative form of the adjective in brackets.

1 You've got _____ less _____ (little) money than me.
2 I think that was _____ (bad) film I've ever seen.
3 My house is _____ (far) from the school than my friend's house.
4 Who got _____ (many) questions wrong in the English test than me?
5 My English marks were _____ (good) than my German marks.
6 However, my history marks were _____ (bad) than my geography marks.
7 Clare ate _____ (much) ice cream than Mae.
8 Of all the groups in the class, Gianni's group did _____ (little) work for the project.

4 Complete the sentences with the superlative form of the adjective in brackets.

1 Who is _____ the youngest _____ (young) person in your family?
2 Linda has got _____ (expensive) trainers of all my friends.
3 My sister is _____ (short) person in my family.
4 Who is _____ (old) person in the world?
5 My bedroom is _____ (tidy) room in the house.
6 The living room is _____ (large) room in the house.
7 You are _____ (lazy) person I know!
8 Our teacher is _____ (funny) teacher in the school.

6 Circle the correct answer.

1 He's the ___ man I've ever seen.
   a the taller   (b) the tallest   c tallest
2 The weather in India is ___ the UK.
   a hotter than   b more hot   c the hottest
3 Jess can speak English ___ Ruth.
   a gooder than   b better than   c best of
4 There are ___ people in England than there are in Scotland.
   a many   b much   c more
5 The River Nile is one of ___ rivers in the world.
   a the longer   b the longest   c longest
6 I ran ___ than my sister in the race.
   a faster   b the faster   c fastest than
7 Greg got ___ marks out of everyone in the class.
   a the better   b best than   c the best
8 My brother is ___ than me.
   a the oldest   b older   c old

132

Comparatives, superlatives and adverbs of manner Unit 19

7 Find the mistakes in the sentences. Then write them correctly.

1 Our classroom is <u>tidiest</u> than theirs.
   <u>Our classroom is tidier than theirs.</u>

2 Jin is the more intelligent boy in our school.
   _____

3 I'm thin than my brother.
   _____

4 Who got the higher mark in English?
   _____

5 That is the bad cake I've ever tasted.
   _____

6 She's the most tall girl in our class.
   _____

7 My cousins' house is more bigger than our house.
   _____

8 This is most comfortable seat in the house.
   _____

Think about it!

Adjectives with one or two syllables usually take -er and -est. Adjectives with more than two syllables take *more* and *most*.

Adverbs of manner

We use adverbs of manner to show the way in which someone does something. Adverbs of manner answer the question *How?*
(How does she sing?)   She sings **beautifully**.
(How does he speak?)   He speaks **quietly**.

We form most adverbs by adding *-ly* to the adjective.
quick   →   quickly

When the adjective ends in *-e*, we usually take off the *-e* and add *-ly*.
gentle   →   gently

When the adjective ends in *-l*, we add *-ly*.
careful   →   carefully

When the adjective ends in *-y*, we take off the *-y* and add *-ily*.
easy   →   easily
happy   →   happily

8 Write the adverbs of manner for these adjectives.

1 nice   <u>   nicely   </u>
2 slow   _____
3 quick   _____
4 careless _____
5 angry   _____
6 quiet   _____
7 excited   _____
8 rude   _____

Unit 19 — Comparatives, superlatives and adverbs of manner

9 Complete the sentences with the adverb form of the adjective in brackets.

1 Please don't speak ___rudely___ (rude) to your friends.
2 Talk to the baby _____ (quiet).
3 I don't want you to play your music _____ (loud).
4 He answered all the questions on the quiz show _____ (easy).
5 Dad drives very _____ (careful).
6 Why is he shouting _____ (angry) at those boys?
7 I think you did those maths exercises _____ (careless).
8 You should eat your food _____ (slow).

Irregular adverbs of manner

Some adverbs are irregular and do not follow these rules.

good → well   late → late
fast → fast   early → early
hard → hard   near → near
high → high

10 Circle the correct answer.

1 He drives his car very *fastly* / *(fast)*.
2 Why did he arrive home *lately* / *late* last night?
3 I can play the piano very *good* / *well*.
4 Look at that kite. It's flying *high* / *higher* than all the others.
5 I'm pleased you got good marks in the test. You worked very *hard* / *hardly*.
6 I'm not very *good* / *well* at art.

11 Complete the sentences with the adverbs from the box.

| ~~angrily~~ | brightly | fast | happily |
| hungrily | politely | quickly | well |

1 The waiter broke all the plates and his boss shouted at him ___angrily___ .
2 The small children played _____ while their parents sat and talked.
3 He ran really _____ , but he didn't win the race.
4 I didn't know you could sing that _____ .
5 In summer, the sun shines _____ .
6 I prefer young people who speak _____ to adults.
7 Give me the phone _____ . We must call an ambulance!
8 We all ate our dinner _____ after we'd been swimming.

12 Find the mistakes in the sentences. Then write them correctly.

1 He spoke so **quiet** that I couldn't hear him properly.
   ___He spoke so quietly that I couldn't hear him properly.___

2 If you're sitting comfortable, I'll tell you a story.
   _____
   _____

3 Hamid has got a big car, but he drives it careful.
   _____
   _____

4 I can only understand you if you speak slowest.
   _____
   _____

5 He sings badly, but he plays the guitar good.
   _____
   _____

6 We can easy win the match.
   _____
   _____

Comparatives, superlatives and adverbs of manner — Unit 19

13 Complete the sentences so the second sentence has a similar meaning to the first.

1 Yasmin is a beautiful dancer.
   Yasmin _____dances beautifully_____ .

2 Those girls are good volleyball players.
   Those girls play _____ .

3 Jim is very careless when he does his homework.
   Jim does his _____ .

4 Meena is always polite when she speaks to her parents.
   Meena always speaks _____ .

5 Daisy is happy when she plays with her friends.
   Daisy plays _____ .

6 Alan is a fast runner when he's in a race.
   Alan runs _____ .

14 Answer the questions in your own words.

1 What do you do badly?
   I sing badly.

2 What do you do happily?
   _____

3 What does your mother do well?
   _____

4 Who is the funniest person you know?
   _____

5 What can you do easily?
   _____

6 What kind of work do you do quickly?
   _____

Pairwork

Work in pairs. Take turns to ask and answer about how you do the things below.

- brush your teeth
- do your homework
- play sports
- eat your food
- comb your hair
- talk to your parents
- behave in class
- speak English
- sleep

For example:
How do you sing? Badly!   How do you walk to school? Slowly.

Writing

Write a short essay about your family. Say as much as you can about each person, and use comparatives and superlatives as much as possible.

135

UNIT 20 Present perfect continuous

Present perfect continuous

Affirmative	Negative	Question
I have (I've) been working	I have not (haven't) been working	Have I been working?
you have (you've) been working	you have not (haven't) been working	Have you been working?
he has (he's) been working	he has not (hasn't) been working	Has he been working?
she has (she's) been working	she has not (hasn't) been working	Has she been working?
it has (it's) been working	it has not (hasn't) been working	Has it been working?
we have (we've) been working	we have not (haven't) been working	Have we been working?
you have (you've) been working	you have not (haven't) been working	Have you been working?
they have (they've) been working	they have not (haven't) been working	Have they been working?

Short answers

Yes, I/you have.   No, I/you haven't.
Yes, he/she/it has.   No, he/she/it hasn't.
Yes, we/you/they have.   No, we/you/they haven't.

We use the present perfect continuous to talk about:

- something that started in the past and that has been repeated or continued until now.
  *How long **have you been living** here?*
  *She**'s been working** all day.*

- something that happened repeatedly or continuously in the past and that may have finished, but we can still see the result now.
  *She**'s been running**. (Her face is red and she looks hot.)*
  *He**'s been mending** the car. (His hands are covered in oil.)*

What has she been doing?

She's been mending her bike since ten o'clock this morning.

Present perfect continuous Unit 20

1 Complete the sentences with the present perfect continuous.

1 Dad ___has been decorating___ (decorate) the living room since eight o'clock.
2 She _____ (listen) to her music all morning.
3 The children _____ (watch) TV for too long.
4 I _____ (ride) horses since I was four.
5 It _____ (rain) for the last ten days.
6 We _____ (wait) for hours.

Think about it!

With the present perfect continuous, we always use *been*.

2 Write questions.

1 you / clean / your bedroom
  Have you been cleaning your bedroom?
2 he / lie / in bed / until now
  _____
3 they / dance / all night
  _____
4 you / study / all morning
  _____
5 it / snow / since last night
  _____
6 he / walk / forest
  _____

3 Make the sentences negative.

1 We've been studying English since we were two years old.
  We haven't been studying English since we were two years old.
2 I've been wearing these clothes since I last saw you.
  _____
3 I have been waiting for a long time.
  _____
4 He has been feeling very well since this morning.
  _____
5 We have been making dinner for two hours.
  _____
6 The baby has been crying for an hour.
  _____

Time expressions

We can use the words *for* and *since* with the present perfect continuous.

for + a period of time (e.g. *a week*, *three days*, etc.)
I'**ve been living** here **for** two years.

since + a point in time (e.g. *last month*, *when I was young*, etc.)
He'**s been driving since** seven o'clock this morning.

4 Complete the sentences with *for* or *since*.

1 They've been watching TV ___since___ nine o'clock this morning.
2 Dad's been working in the bank _____ 2011.
3 He's been decorating our house _____ three weeks.
4 I've been listening carefully to the teacher _____ the last two hours.
5 We've been living in this house _____ we built it.
6 He's been doing the housework _____ hours!

137

Unit 20 Present perfect continuous

5 Tick (✓) the correct sentence, a or b.

1. a The sun's been shining for all day. ___
   b The sun's been shining all day. ✓
2. a He's been painting pictures since he was thirteen. ___
   b He's been painting pictures for he was thirteen. ___
3. a Dad's been cleaning the kitchen for ages. ___
   b Dad's been cleaning the kitchen since ages. ___
4. a We've been travel all night. ___
   b We've been travelling all night. ___
5. a She's been climbing mountains since she was a young girl. ___
   b She's be climbing mountains since she was a young girl. ___
6. a They have been dance for hours. ___
   b They have been dancing for hours. ___

6 Match 1–6 with a–f. Then write sentences.

1. There are dirty saucepans and bowls in the kitchen.
2. There is a wet towel and swimsuit on the chair.
3. There are trainers and shorts on the floor.
4. There are tins of paint and brushes on the table.
5. There are a lot of papers on the desk.
6. There are wet coats and boots in the hall.

a. She has been swimming.
b. I've been decorating my room.
c. It has been raining.
d. The teacher has been working.
e. Cara has been running.
f. Dad has been making dinner.

1. There are dirty saucepans and bowls in the kitchen. Dad has been making dinner.
2. _____
3. _____
4. _____
5. _____
6. _____

7 Circle the correct answer.

1. They haven't ___ speaking to each other for days.
   a to   b (been)   c be
2. Tim has been ___ for a new job since last year.
   a looking   b look   c looked
3. Scientists have been studying the planet Mars ___ many years.
   a since   b after   c for
4. ___ they been studying hard all morning?
   a Are   b Have   c Did
5. The comedian has been telling jokes ___ evening.
   a for   b since   c all
6. Mum has been cutting the grass ___ she went outside.
   a for   b after   c since

138

Present perfect continuous — Unit 20

8 Write the words in the correct order.

1. for / has / she / exercising / hours / been / two
   She has been exercising for two hours.

2. since / have / hard / been / breakfast / working / they / ?
   _____

3. this / years / has / she / for / doing / been / job
   _____

4. my / been / who / phone / has / using / ?
   _____

5. long / been / we / living / haven't / here / for
   _____

6. was / been / I / sixteen / golf / playing / have / since / I
   _____

9 Answer the questions in your own words.

1. How long have you been living in your house?
   I have been living in my house since
   I was born.

2. How long have you been learning English?
   _____

3. How long have you been having lessons with this English teacher?
   _____

4. What have you been doing today?
   _____

5. What grammar point have you been studying in your English class this week?
   _____

6. How long have you been going to this school?
   _____

Pairwork

Work in pairs. Talk about some of the things you have been doing since you were young and some of the things you have only been doing for a short time.

For example:

I've been living in my town since I was four years old.
I've been learning Spanish for two months.
I've been going to the cinema with my friends since last year.

Writing

Imagine that every week you and your friend send emails to each other, telling each other what you've been doing. Write this week's email to your friend. Include what you have been doing:

- at school.
- at home.
- in your free time.
- at the weekend.

139

Grammar review 5   Units 17–20

1 Complete the sentences using gerunds.

1 __Driving__ (drive) a car can be dangerous.
2 My brothers both hate _____ (swim).
3 Dad goes _____ (run) every morning.
4 Her hobbies include _____ (cook) and karate.
5 My grandma spends a lot of time _____ (sew).
6 She's very good at Latin American _____ (dance).
7 _____ (ride) a horse is good exercise.
8 _____ (eat) fruit and vegetables is good for your health.

2 Complete the sentences with the verbs from the box. Use gerunds.

| act | check | ~~eat~~ | help | join | listen | see | wait |

1 My friends love ___eating___ Chinese food.
2 Are you interested in _____ an environmental group?
3 I can't stand _____ in long queues.
4 I really miss _____ my English school friends now that I live in France.
5 My sister is very good at _____. She is in a theatre group.
6 She doesn't like _____ to loud rock music.
7 They don't mind _____ us to do the housework.
8 We never go away without _____ the weather forecast first.

3 Circle the correct answer.

1 He has given up ___ cakes and sweets.
   a to eat   b eat   (c) eating
2 I was surprised ___ that I got the best marks in the class.
   a to find out   b finding out   c found out
3 I would be happy ___ help you with your project.
   a in   b to   c for
4 She's keen on ___ how to water ski.
   a to learn   b learns   c learning
5 The teacher won't allow her ___ the day off.
   a taking   b to take   c take
6 I've decided ___ art at university.
   a to study   b studying   c for to study
7 I want ___ to New Zealand next year.
   a to go   b going   c to be gone
8 We love ___ English!
   a learn   b learning   c to learning

4 Find the extra word and write it in the space.

1 I love to having a hot shower every morning. ___to___
2 Millie loves for meeting her friends in town for coffee. _____
3 Do you like some listening to classical music? _____
4 I'm bored with it hearing about your problems every day! _____
5 We love to watch the dolphins are playing in the sea. _____
6 She promised to be give me the money back soon. _____

Units 17–20 **Grammar review 5**

5 Complete the sentences with *is* or *are*.
1. Formula One cars _____are_____ driven by expert drivers.
2. Lots of tea _____ grown in China.
3. Many songs _____ played on the radio every day.
4. BMW cars _____ made in Germany.
5. Some rare animals _____ kept in zoos.
6. My shoes _____ made of leather.
7. My bag _____ made of cotton.
8. The World Cup _____ watched by millions of people every four years.

6 Complete the sentences with *was* or *were*.
1. The teacher _____was_____ given a huge bunch of flowers by her students.
2. Those flowers _____ picked from my garden.
3. Mount Everest _____ climbed by Sir Edmund Hilary.
4. The tennis match _____ seen by millions of people.
5. The Giza Pyramids _____ built by the ancient Egyptians.
6. The painting called *Sunflowers* _____ painted by Vincent Van Gogh.
7. Television _____ invented by John Logie Baird.
8. Our house _____ sold last year.

7 Change the sentences from active to passive.
1. The Inuit build igloos.
   Igloos are built by the Inuit.
2. Did a friend of yours design this bracelet?
   _____
3. Someone makes these T-shirts in India.
   _____
4. Amal didn't cut the grass.
   _____
5. A fire caused the damage.
   _____
6. J.R.R. Tolkien wrote *The Hobbit*.
   _____
7. Did your uncle make this table?
   _____
8. Architects designed this house.
   _____

Grammar review 5   Units 17–20

8 Complete the sentences with the comparative form of the adjective in brackets.

1. I am ____shorter____ (short) than my sister.
2. He works _____ (hard) than anybody I know.
3. Do you think skiing is _____ (dangerous) than driving?
4. Fruit is _____ (good) for you than chocolate.
5. Is your dad _____ (tall) than your mum?
6. My headache is _____ (bad) than it was an hour ago.
7. My bike is _____ (fast) than his.
8. I think you're _____ (intelligent) than me!

9 Complete the sentences with the superlative form of the adjective in brackets.

1. That's __the biggest__ (big) cake I've ever seen.
2. My English teacher is _____ (nice) person in the school!
3. Are elephants _____ (strong) animals in the world?
4. What's _____ (bad) mark you've ever had?
5. She's _____ (happy) baby I've ever seen.
6. Which dinosaur was _____ (large)?
7. They make _____ (good) pizza in Italy!
8. What's _____ (exciting) thing you've ever done?

10 Circle the correct answer.

1. She's got longer hair ___ me.
   a of   b than   c as   *(b circled)*
2. That's ___ most beautiful view of the city.
   a the   b than   c a
3. What could be ___ enjoyable than lying on the beach?
   a most   b more   c as
4. Who got the ___ marks in the exam?
   a low   b lower   c lowest
5. Can cheetahs run ___ than lions?
   a fastest   b faster   c fast
6. What is the ___ expensive thing in the shop?
   a most   b more   c little

11 Complete the sentences with the adverb form of the adjective in brackets.

1. We waited ____patiently____ (patient) for the teacher to arrive.
2. The boy ran _____ (quick) down the road.
3. My head hurts – don't play your drums so _____ (loud)!
4. They laughed _____ (happy) at the boy telling jokes.
5. She checked the money _____ (careful).
6. Why are you driving so _____ (fast)?
7. I wish you would sing more _____ (quiet)!
8. Why is he shouting so _____ (angry)?

Units 17–20 **Grammar review 5**

12 Complete the sentences with the present perfect continuous.
1 She _____has been living_____ (live) in Norway since 2014.
2 The birds _____ (feed) their babies.
3 The rain _____ (fall) for hours.
4 The cat _____ (hunt) for mice.
5 _____ the rabbit _____ (dig) holes?
6 We _____ (study) all morning.
7 _____ the boys _____ (play) all afternoon?
8 They _____ (talk) for hours.

13 Circle the correct answer.
1 He ___ learning to drive for six months.
   a has been   b is   c was being
2 The computer has not ___ working for three days.
   a be   b been   c being
3 Why have you been ___ at everybody today?
   a shouting   b shouted   c shouts
4 I've ___ learning to swim this summer.
   a been   b being   c be
5 He's been waiting for you ___ this afternoon.
   a for   b at   c since
6 Dad has been reading the same book for ___ .
   a weeks   b nine o'clock   c all evening
7 I've been sleeping ___ night.
   a for   b since   c all
8 She's been playing the drums ___ years.
   a since   b for   c in

14 Find the extra word and write it in the space.
1 Where have they the children been playing? _____they_____
2 How long for have you been living in Toronto? _____
3 She has been talking on the phone for thirty minutes ago. _____
4 The baby it has been crying all day. _____
5 What has Dan been doing since at school all day? _____
6 We haven't are been waiting for very long. _____
7 People have and been using computers for many years. _____
8 How long for has it been raining? _____

Writing 1   Description: writing about your favourite person

1 Find the opposites and write them on the lines.

1 husband ≠	wife
2 fat ≠	
3 short ≠	
4 straight ≠	
5 sad ≠	
6 son ≠	

2 Read Jade's description. Write *T* for true or *F* for false.

My favourite person

My grandma is my favourite person. Her name's Ellen and she's sixty years old. She lives in the same town as us. She hasn't got any brothers or sisters.

Grandma's short. She isn't thin, but she isn't fat either. She's got short grey hair. It's very curly! She's got lovely brown eyes. She wears glasses when she reads.

I spend a lot of time with my grandma. I often go to her house after school, and sometimes we go for a walk in the park. We talk and laugh a lot. I tell her all my secrets because she gives really great advice.

My grandma is a happy person and she always smiles. She's very kind and I love her very much.

1	Ellen is Jade's granddaughter.	F
2	Ellen's hair is short and curly.	___
3	Jade's grandma lives with Jade.	___
4	Ellen's eyes are grey.	___
5	Sometimes Jade's grandma wears glasses.	___
6	Ellen and Jade sometimes go to the park.	___

3 Read again. In which paragraph does Jade

1	describe what her grandma looks like?	2
2	say what she does with her grandma?	___
3	say who her favourite person is?	___
4	say how she feels about her grandma?	___

Description: writing about your favourite person **Writing 1**

4 **Complete Jade's writing plan.**

Title:	My favourite person
Paragraph 1:	¹ _____say who my favourite person is_____ , say what her name is and how old she is, say where she lives, say what family she has got
Paragraph 2:	² _____
Paragraph 3:	³ _____
Paragraph 4:	say what kind of person she is, ⁴ _____

5 **Read another description. Complete the description with the verbs from the box. Use the present simple.**

> carry   have got   ~~live~~   love   play   ride   sit   spend

My favourite person

My favourite person is Joe. He's my best friend and he's ten years old, like me. Joe ¹ _____lives_____ in my street and he ² _____ next to me at school. He's got one brother and one sister.

Joe's tall and thin. He ³ _____ big blue eyes and short hair. He ⁴ _____ sweets and he always ⁵ _____ some in his pocket!

Joe and I ⁶ _____ a lot of time together. We both like sports and music, and we often ⁷ _____ the drums together. At the weekend, we ⁸ _____ our bikes in the park. I'm faster than him!

Joe's a great friend. He's a very nice person and we have lots of fun.

Now it's your turn!

6 **Use Jade's writing plan to make notes for your description of your favourite person below.**

My writing plan notes	
Title:	_____
Paragraph 1:	_____
Paragraph 2:	_____
Paragraph 3:	_____
Paragraph 4:	_____

7 **Now use your writing plan to write a description of your favourite person. Write in your notebook.**

Writing 2

Story: narrative about an event involving free-time activities

1 Match 1–5 with a–e.

1 My brother was playing volleyball on Sunday.
2 Dad usually plays golf on Fridays.
3 Suki often goes running on Saturdays.
4 My family and I went for a walk last week.
5 Liz loves music.

a While we were having a picnic, it started raining.
b When I saw her at the sports centre, she was running in a race.
c Yesterday, he stayed at home because it was raining.
d She was playing the trumpet when I got to her house.
e He's the best player in the team.

2 Read Ken's story. Answer the questions.

My Saturday

I have got a lot of free time at the weekend and I enjoy being outside. On Saturday mornings, I often go running at the sports centre. I am very fast and I often win races. In the afternoon, I usually ride my bike, and I sometimes play basketball with my friends in the evening.

Last Saturday was different! When I woke up, it was raining. I went into the kitchen and my dad, who usually plays golf in the morning, was reading my favourite comic. Mum often goes to the swimming pool, but she was listening to music. My sister Lin, who never stays at home on Saturdays, was watching TV, and my baby brother was playing with his toys.

Everyone was having a nice time. I decided to stay at home too. We have always got lots of things to do at the weekend and it was nice to be at home together. In the afternoon, I was playing the piano when Lin came and sat next to me. We sang songs together and we had a lot of fun!

1 What does Ken often do on Saturday mornings?
   goes running at the sports centre
2 What was the weather like last Saturday?
   _____
3 What does Ken's dad usually do on Saturday mornings?
   _____
4 What was Lin doing?
   _____
5 Why did Ken want to be at home?
   _____
6 What was Ken doing when Lin came and sat next to him?
   _____

3 Read again. In which paragraph does Ken say

1 what his family did last Saturday?   ___
2 what he usually does on Saturdays?   ___
3 what he did last Saturday?   ___

Story: narrative about an event involving free-time activities — **Writing 2**

4 Complete Ken's writing plan.

Paragraph 1:	¹ _____ on Saturdays in my free time
Paragraph 2:	² _____ which made last Saturday different
Paragraph 3:	say what I ³ _____ last Saturday

5 Read another story. Use the notes to write the missing sentences.

1 when / he / arrive / I / read / magazine / my room
2 they / cook / lunch
3 it / come / from / sister's room
4 Tim / play / drums / Carol / dance
5 we / have / a lot / fun

My Sunday

Sunday is usually a very quiet day. I tidy my room and then I meet my friends. We usually go to the park together. In the afternoon, I usually read comics and I sometimes play table tennis.

Last Sunday was different! My cousin Tim came to visit.
¹ When he arrived, I was reading a comic in my room.
My sister Carol was riding her bike outside. Mum and Dad were in the kitchen.
² _____ Suddenly, I heard a loud noise.
³ _____ I went upstairs and opened the door to Carol's room. ⁴ _____

I decided to stay with them and sing my favourite song.
⁵ _____ My parents came upstairs and started laughing at us. It was very funny! We had a great time.

Now it's your turn!

6 Use Ken's writing plan to make notes for your story about a day with your family below.

| My writing plan notes |
| Paragraph 1: _____ |
| Paragraph 2: _____ |
| Paragraph 3: _____ |

7 Now use your writing plan to write a story about a day with your family. Write in your notebook.

Writing 3 — Story: describing a day out (seasonal weather, actions and feelings)

1 Complete the crossword about weather in the UK.

Down
1. We can't see many things on a _____ day.
2. January is in _____ .
3. The _____ is blue in July.
4. Be careful! There's _____ on the ground.
5. The leaves are brown and orange in _____ .
8. Don't go sailing! There's going to be a _____ .

Across
3. In _____ , we see pretty flowers.
6. The sky is _____ when it's raining.
7. You don't need a coat in _____ weather.
8. _____ is the hottest season.

2 Read Ana's story. Write *T* for true or *F* for false.

An exciting spring day

Last week, my parents decided to take my brother and me for a day out. We woke up early on Saturday morning. It was a warm, sunny day. Mum made some sandwiches and we got into the car at half past nine.

One hour later, we were in the forest. There were pretty flowers everywhere and the birds were singing. There were some clouds and Mum said, 'We haven't brought an umbrella, but it hasn't rained for weeks.' We got out of the car and went for a walk. Suddenly, I heard a loud noise. I looked up at the sky. It wasn't blue anymore and the sun wasn't shining. It was cloudy. 'Look at those clouds. There's going to be a storm!' my brother said. It started raining and we ran to the car. We were all wet and cold.

On our way home, the sun came out again. There weren't many clouds in the sky. 'Look! There's a rainbow,' Mum said. 'I've never seen a huge rainbow like that,' my brother said. We stopped the car near a lake and had a picnic before we went home. It was a great day!

1. Ana and her family went on a trip on Saturday. __T__
2. When they left home, it was sunny. ___
3. Ana's mum took an umbrella with her. ___
4. When they got to the forest, there were lots of clouds in the sky. ___
5. After they got wet, it was sunny again. ___
6. They saw a rainbow when they got home. ___

3 Read again. In which paragraph does Ana say

1. what they did in the end? ___
2. what the weather was like when they got up? ___
3. what happened to them when they got to the forest? ___

Story: describing a day out (seasonal weather, actions and feelings) — **Writing 3**

4 **Complete Ana's writing plan.**

Paragraph 1: say where we decided to go, ¹ _____

Paragraph 2: describe the forest, say what the weather was like in the forest,
² _____

Paragraph 3: say what we saw, ³ _____

5 **Read another story. Complete the story with the phrases from the box.**

> ~~We haven't been to the mountains this winter~~
> Let's make a snowman
> it was really foggy
> Then my aunt threw a snowball at me
> Our journey to the mountains took
> there was ice on the road

An exciting winter day

A month ago, my uncle and aunt decided to take my brother and me skiing in the mountains. ¹'<u>We haven't been to the mountains this winter</u>,' my uncle said. We woke up early on Saturday morning. It was cold and the sky was grey. We had breakfast and left.

² _____ one and a half hours. My aunt drove slowly because ³ _____. When we got to the mountains, nobody was skiing. We couldn't see anything because ⁴ _____. 'What shall we do now?' my uncle asked.

My brother had an idea. ⁵ '_____,' he said. 'I've never made one before.' We all agreed that this was a great idea.
⁶ _____. I threw one at her and one at my brother too. We've never laughed so much together! It was a very exciting day.

Now it's your turn!

6 **Use Ana's writing plan to make notes for your story about a day out in summer or autumn below.**

My writing plan notes
Paragraph 1: _____
Paragraph 2: _____
Paragraph 3: _____

7 **Now use your writing plan to write a story about an exciting day out in summer or autumn. Write in your notebook.**

Writing 4 — Letter: writing to a friend about plans for a shopping trip and a visit

1 Find and write.

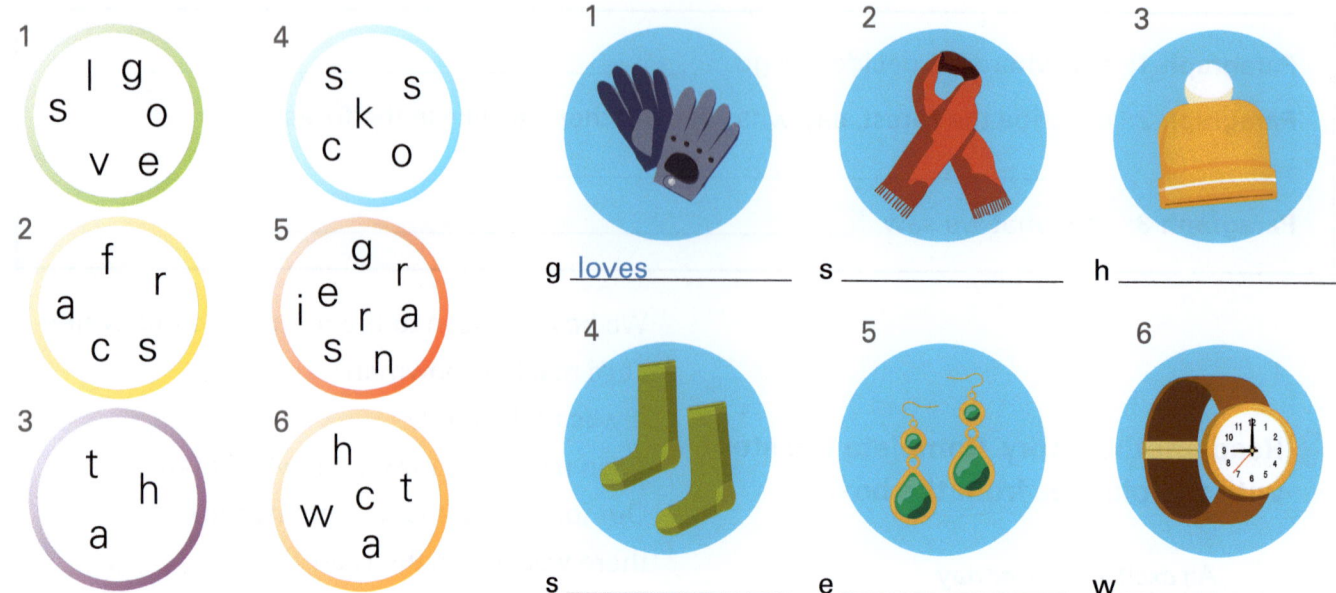

1. g _loves_
2. s _____
3. h _____
4. s _____
5. e _____
6. w _____

2 Read Andrew's letter. Answer the questions.

Dear Viktor,

How are you? I'm writing to tell you that next week I'm going to London to visit my grandparents. It's Grandpa's birthday.

On Saturday morning, we're going to go to a shopping centre on Oxford Street. You know I don't like shopping very much, but I want to get Grandpa a nice present. I'm going to buy him a grey woollen scarf and gloves. I hope he likes them. I'm going to go to a bookshop too, because I've seen a new book that Grandma wants to read. She loves reading.

On Saturday evening, we're going to have a party for Grandpa. He doesn't know about it. We've invited his friends and all the family. Grandma's going to make the birthday cake. It'll be a huge chocolate cake. We're also going to buy lots of other nice things to eat. I can't wait! We're going to have a great time.

That's all for now. Write soon and tell me your news.

Love,
Andrew

1. Who is Andrew visiting next week? _____ _his grandparents_ _____
2. Where is Andrew going to go on Saturday morning? _____
3. What present does Andrew want to buy for his grandpa? _____
4. Why is he going to go to the bookshop? _____
5. Who's going to be at the party? _____
6. What's Andrew's grandma going to do? _____

3 Read again. In which paragraph does Andrew say

1. what he's going to do on Saturday evening? ___
2. why he's writing the letter? ___
3. what he's going to buy? ___

Letter: writing to a friend about plans for a shopping trip and a visit — **Writing 4**

4 Complete Andrew's writing plan.

Greeting:	Dear …
Paragraph 1:	say ¹ _____ and where I'm going next week
Paragraph 2:	say where I'm going to go shopping, ² _____
Paragraph 3:	³ _____ , say what other things I'll do at the party
Ending:	That's all for now. Write soon and tell me your news.
Sign off:	Love …

5 Read another letter. Divide it into paragraphs.

Dear Tony,

How are you? I'm writing to tell you that I'm visiting my cousins in Liverpool next weekend, just before school starts! On Friday, I'm going to go to the big supermarket in my neighbourhood. I like going there because the shop assistants are very friendly. I'll get a pair of shorts for Tom and a pair of silver earrings for Kathy. I don't know what to buy for my aunt and uncle! Last year, I gave my aunt a pair of gloves and I got a book for my uncle. My cousins and I will go to the autumn bazaar at Kathy's school on Saturday. It's great because you can buy really cheap things there. We're also going to go to the cinema. We're going to see an animated film. I can't wait! We're going to have a great time together. That's all for now. Write and tell me what you're doing at the weekend.

Love,

Leena

Now it's your turn!

6 Imagine you are going to spend the weekend at your friend's house. Use Andrew's writing plan to help you make notes for your letter to your cousin below.

My writing plan notes

Greeting: _____
Paragraph 1: _____
Paragraph 2: _____
Paragraph 3: _____
Ending: _____
Sign off: _____

7 Now use your writing plan to write a letter about next weekend. Write in your notebook.

Writing 5 — Article: writing about things to do with school

1 Complete the words about school.

THINGS TO DO

¹ s <u>c i e n c</u> e

Study for the ² e _ _ _.

English

Bring a ³ d _ _ t _ _ _ _ r _ to find new words.

Write an article about my favourite ⁴ s _ _ j _ _ t at school.

Correct my spelling ⁵ m _ _ t _ _ es.

⁶ g _ o _ _ _ _ p _ _

Learn the names of all the countries in Africa.

Find out how many different ⁷ l _ _ g u _ _ e _ people speak there.

art

Bring ⁸ s _ _ _ _ s _ _ _ s to cut out pictures for the competition.

2 Read Nicky's article. Write *T* for true or *F* for false.

Why are dictionaries important?

Can you use a dictionary? Some pupils don't think they're useful, but I don't agree. I think dictionaries can help us to learn about our language and other languages.

First of all, when you read a book, you can find out the meanings of new words in a dictionary. You'll be able to use these words in your writing and it'll be a lot more interesting. You can spell words correctly, too. It's nice when your homework isn't full of spelling mistakes!

Now you can understand why it's a good idea to use a dictionary. You can probably find a dictionary in your school library, but the quickest way to look up new words is to use a good online dictionary or a dictionary app. These are easy to use, and a lot of them are free!

1 Nicky agrees with pupils who don't like dictionaries. <u>F</u>
2 Dictionaries help us with different languages. ___
3 A dictionary can help you to understand new words. ___
4 When you use a dictionary, you can use more words in your writing. ___
5 You can find lots of spelling mistakes in dictionaries. ___
6 Nicky says pupils must buy dictionaries. ___

3 Read again. In which paragraph does Nicky

1 give advice to the reader? ___
2 say why it's good to use a dictionary? ___
3 say what she thinks? ___

Article: writing about things to do with school   Writing 5

4 Complete Nicky's writing plan.

Title: Why are dictionaries important?
Paragraph 1: ¹ _____, starting with a question
Paragraph 2: give two reasons ² _____
Paragraph 3: end the article, ³ _____ to the reader

5 Read another article. Put the paragraphs in the correct order by writing 1–3 on the lines.

Why are exams important?

a ___ Do you like exams? My school friends hate them, but I think we need exams at school. They're very important for students and for teachers.

b ___ Now you can understand why it's a good idea to do exams. Don't worry about your exams. Study hard and you'll be ready to get a good mark.

c ___ Exams give us a reason to study more. They also help teachers to see how much you have learnt from your lessons. If you don't do well in an exam, the teacher knows what you don't understand and helps you to learn better. Then you'll get a better mark the next time you do an exam.

Now it's your turn!

6 Use Nicky's writing plan to make notes for your article about why homework is important below.

My writing plan notes
Title: _____
Paragraph 1: _____
Paragraph 2: _____
Paragraph 3: _____

7 Now use your writing plan to write an article about why homework is important. Write in your notebook.

Writing 6 — Email: writing about a health problem

1 Find and write.

1 e _arache_   2 c _____   3 h _____
4 t _____   5 t _____   6 s _____
a _____

2 Read Jack's email. Write T for true or F for false.

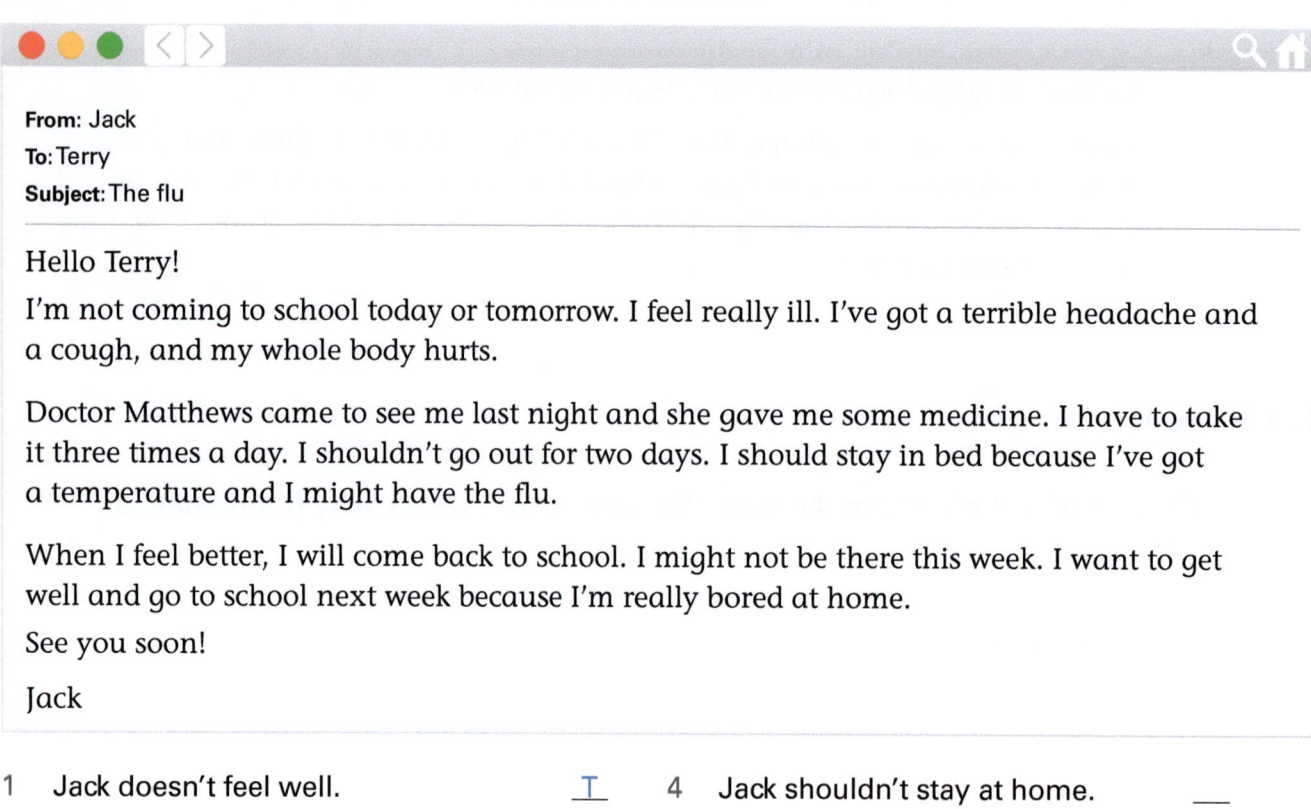

From: Jack
To: Terry
Subject: The flu

Hello Terry!

I'm not coming to school today or tomorrow. I feel really ill. I've got a terrible headache and a cough, and my whole body hurts.

Doctor Matthews came to see me last night and she gave me some medicine. I have to take it three times a day. I shouldn't go out for two days. I should stay in bed because I've got a temperature and I might have the flu.

When I feel better, I will come back to school. I might not be there this week. I want to get well and go to school next week because I'm really bored at home.

See you soon!

Jack

1 Jack doesn't feel well. __T__
2 Jack's head hurts. ___
3 Doctor Matthews visited Jack at home. ___
4 Jack shouldn't stay at home. ___
5 Jack hasn't got a temperature. ___
6 Jack doesn't want to stay at home. ___

3 Read again. In which paragraph does Jack say

1 what the matter is and how he feels? ___
2 when he might come back to school? ___
3 what he should and shouldn't do? ___

Writing 6

Email: writing about a health problem

4 **Complete Jack's writing plan.**

Greeting:	Hello … !
Paragraph 1:	say I'm not coming to school, say ¹ _____
Paragraph 2:	say what the doctor did and what she gave me, say ² _____
Paragraph 3:	say ³ _____ , say how I feel at home

5 **Read another email. Circle the correct answer.**

1 **a** couldn't **b** can't **c** haven't   4 **a** should **b** shouldn't **c** may
2 **a** am   **b** had   **c** was   5 **a** might   **b** have   **c** was
3 **a** was   **b** should **c** may   6 **a** was   **b** had   **c** may

---

Hello Sally!

I'm sorry I ¹ _____ come to your party last night. I was ill. I ² _____ terrible toothache and my head hurt too.

I went to the dentist this morning. He fixed my tooth and gave me some medicine. I have to take it twice a day and I ³ _____ be careful what I eat. I ⁴ _____ eat anything for a few hours and I should just drink a lot. I ⁵ _____ go to see the dentist again tomorrow if my tooth still hurts.

I feel better now. I should be fine this weekend and I ⁶ _____ come and see you then.

See you soon!
Molly

Now it's your turn!

6 **Imagine that you've been ill and you can't go swimming with a friend. Use Jack's writing plan to make notes for your email below.**

My writing plan notes	
Greeting:	_____
Paragraph 1:	_____
Paragraph 2:	_____
Paragraph 3:	_____
Ending:	_____
Sign off:	_____

7 **Now use your writing plan to write an email to your friend explaining that you are ill and you can't go swimming.**

Writing 7 — Letter of invitation: writing about plans for a party and inviting

1 Find and write.

I have to put the ¹ p asta_____ on the top shelf of the cupboard and the
² b _____ on the bottom shelf, next to the sugar. The ³ t _____ goes on the
middle shelf, next to the ⁴ j _____ . I'll put the ⁵ s _____ on the cooker, and
then I can make the sauce in it. The ⁶ v _____ on the big plate go in the middle of the
table. The ⁷ s _____ has to go in the bowl, and I have to put the ⁸ k _____
on the small plate. I think that's it!

2 Read Jane's letter of invitation. Answer the questions.

Dear Michelle,

How are you? I'm having a party next Friday. It's going to be a different kind of party. It'll be great. You must come.

We're going to cook together! We're going to make a pizza and a chocolate cake. I know you love pizza! Mum and I are going to the supermarket today. We have to buy some cheese, tomatoes and onions for the pizza. We also have to buy eggs, flour, sugar and butter for the cake. Mum's going to help us in the kitchen. We'll have lots of fun. I can't wait!

Remember, you don't have to eat anything before you come. There'll be lots of food and we'll have to eat it all!

See you soon.

Jane

1 When is Jane having a party?
   _____next Friday_____

2 What are Jane are her friends going to do at the party?
   _____

3 What are they going to make?
   _____

4 What do Jane and her mum have to buy for the pizza?
   _____

5 What do they have to buy for the cake?
   _____

6 Why does Jane say Michelle doesn't have to eat before she comes?
   _____

3 Read again. In which paragraph does Jane

1 say what they'll do at the party?   ___
2 say what her friend doesn't have to do?   ___
3 invite her friend to the party?   ___

Letter of invitation: writing about plans for a party and inviting **Writing 7**

4 **Complete Jane's writing plan.**

Greeting: Dear ... ,
Paragraph 1: say where the party is and when, ¹ _____
Paragraph 2: ² _____ , say what we have to buy
Paragraph 3: ³ _____ before she comes to the party and why
Ending: See you soon.

5 **Read another letter of invitation. Complete the letter with the phrases from the box.**

> Mum and I are going to go to the shops
> ~~I'm writing to invite you to~~
> and Dad's going to make the cake
> we're all going to cook
> and we'll have to eat it all
> We also have to buy carrots

Dear Pat,

How are you? ¹ _____I'm writing to invite you to_____ my house next Saturday. Mum and Dad are having a different kind of party and ² _____ . It will be fun! You must come.

Mum, you and I are going to cook some of the food, ³ _____ .
We're going to make pasta with chicken, a bean salad and a carrot cake.
⁴ _____ on Saturday morning to buy chicken for the pasta and beans for the salad. ⁵ _____ , flour and sugar for the cake.

Don't eat too much on Saturday before you come. There will be lots of delicious food,
⁶ _____ !

See you soon.
Tom

Now it's your turn!

6 **Imagine you are your family are having a party on Saturday evening. Use Jane's writing plan to make notes for your letter of invitation below.**

My writing plan notes

Greeting: _____
Paragraph 1: _____
Paragraph 2: _____
Paragraph 3: _____
Ending: _____
Sign off: _____

7 **Now use your writing plan to write a letter of invitation to your party. Write in your notebook.**

Writing 8 Leaflet: writing about an environmental club

1 Complete the crossword.

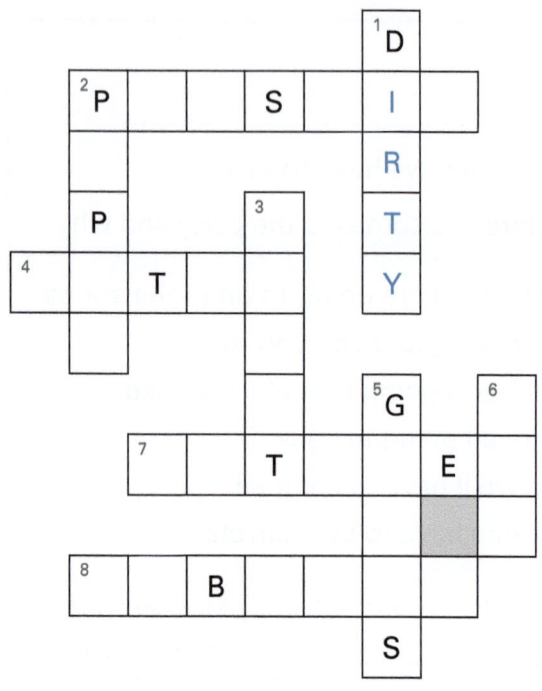

Down

1. Our street is very _____. We must clean it.
2. We must try to save _____ at school.
3. We need to _____ more trees in the city.
5. We've got a _____ table in our kitchen.
6. Don't write on your books! Other students can _____ them next year.

Across

2. We should all try to use less _____.
4. The bin isn't wooden; it's _____.
7. Take your empty _____ back to the shop when you finish your drinks.
8. We must try to use our _____ again.

2 Read Bill's leaflet. Write *T* for true or *F* for false.

Save Our ENVIRONMENT Club

1 What's the problem?

There are fewer trees in the forest and in our streets now than there were a few years ago. People have cut them down to build houses. This damages our environment and our health. If you want to help, please join the Save Our Environment Club.

2 What are we going to do?

We've decided to go to Westfield Forest to plant new trees. We've got lots of trees to plant. If you have some free time, why not come and help us?

3 What can you do if you're interested?

Write your name on the piece of paper on the door outside the geography classroom, if you are interested. Then, meet us in the classroom on Saturday 23rd March at 9:30 a.m.

1. The problem is that people cut down too many trees.   T
2. There aren't any trees in the street.   ___
3. People in the club are going to cut down old trees.   ___
4. There are a lot of new trees for people to plant.   ___
5. Anyone who's interested should go to the geography lesson.   ___
6. They're meeting at Westfield Forest.   ___

3 Read again. In which paragraph does Bill say

1. where and when they're going to meet?   ___
2. what they've decided to do?   ___
3. what the problem is?   ___

Leaflet: writing about an environmental club — Writing 8

4 **Complete Bill's writing plan.**

Title: Save Our Environment Club
Paragraph 1: say ¹ _____
Paragraph 2: say ² _____
Paragraph 3: say what people should do if they're interested and say
             ³ _____

5 **Read another leaflet. Write the headings from the box in the correct place.**

> What have we decided to do?
> What's the problem?
> What can you do if you want to help?

Our Environment Needs Us Club

1 _____

The park by the river is lovely. There are beautiful trees and plants, but it's very dirty. Many people go on picnics there, but there aren't enough bins for the rubbish. Lots of it falls on the ground. When it's windy, the rubbish goes everywhere.

2 _____

The Our Environment Needs Us Club has decided to go to the park and pick up the rubbish. If you have some free time, please come and join us. There's lots of rubbish on the ground and we need lots of people to help.

3 _____

If you want to help, meet us outside the park, on Sunday 11th April at 10:30 in the morning. We've got lots of bags for the rubbish – just remember to wear gloves! Let's clean up the park and make it a nice place for everyone in our neighbourhood.

Now it's your turn!

6 **Imagine that you are in a club called Help the Environment. Use Bill's writing plan to make notes for your leaflet below.**

My writing plan notes

Title: _____
Paragraph 1: _____
Paragraph 2: _____
Paragraph 3: _____

7 **Now use your writing plan to write an information leaflet about your club. Write in your notebook.**

Writing 9 — Diary entry: writing about a school visit to a workplace

1 Match 1–8 with a–h.

1 actor
2 astronaut
3 artist
4 firefighter
5 footballer
6 journalist
7 police officer
8 pilot

a This person is brave and catches thieves.
b This person plays in a team.
c This person works in the theatre or on TV.
d A plane is flown by this person.
e Articles are written by this person.
f This person stops fires burning and saves people.
g Pictures are painted by this person.
h This person travels in space.

2 Read Suzie's diary. Answer the questions.

Friday 23rd September

Today I visited a police station with my class. It was unbelievable! We learnt all about the jobs which are done there.

We all met in front of the school, where a bus was waiting to take us to the police station. When we got there, a police officer showed us around the building. It was very busy! Then we met Nick Peterson, who is a police officer. He took us into his office and he let us sit at his desk and answer the phone. It was very exciting! After that, he gave us police hats to try on. I looked really cool!

The most exciting part of our day was just before we left. We were taken to see the police cars and motorbikes. I'll never forget this visit. Now I want to be a police officer and wear a smart uniform.

1 Where did Suzie and her classmates go today?
    to a police station
2 How did they get there?
    _____
3 What happened when they arrived at the police station?
    _____
4 What did they do in Nick's office?
    _____
5 What did they try on?
    _____
6 What does Suzie want to be when she grows up?
    _____

3 Read again. In which paragraph does Suzie say

1 what the most exciting part of the day was? ___
2 where she went? ___
3 what she did at the police station? ___

Diary entry: writing about a school visit to a workplace Writing 9

4 Complete Suzie's writing plan.

> Date: ...
>
> **Paragraph 1:** say ¹ _____ and who I went with
>
> **Paragraph 2:** say how I got there, ² _____
>
> **Paragraph 3:** ³ _____ , say how I feel about the visit

5 Read another diary entry. Put the paragraphs in the correct order by writing 1–3 on the lines.

> Monday 21st April
>
> a ___ We all met at the station and we went to the stadium by train. When we arrived, we went into a big room, which had pictures of all the players on the wall. We also saw pictures of all their games. Then we put on football shorts and T-shirts with the team's colours. We went outside and ran with the team for an hour. I was really tired. Footballers have to run a lot.
>
> b ___ Then the most amazing things happened. We played football with the team. After the game, they gave us new footballs for our school. All the footballers wrote their names on the footballs. Now I want to be a footballer too and play football all over the world.
>
> c ___ Today was the best day of my life! My classmates and I visited the local football stadium and met our favourite football players.

Now it's your turn!

6 Use Suzie's writing plan to make notes for your diary entry about a school visit to a place where people work below.

> My writing plan notes
>
> Date: _____
>
> Paragraph 1: _____
>
> Paragraph 2: _____
>
> Paragraph 3: _____

7 Now use your writing plan to write a diary entry about a school visit to a place where people work. Write in your notebook.

Writing 10 — Composition (narrative): writing about a project using clothes to help others

1 Circle the correct answer.

1 I must remember *(to fix)* / *fixing* the zip on my trousers.
2 I enjoy *wearing* / *to wear* my new brown belt with the trousers.
3 I'll take my tracksuit because Marie and I both enjoy *jogging* / *to jog*.
4 I want *packing* / *to pack* my trainers.
5 I've decided *taking* / *to take* my new black boots.
6 I should take my raincoat because it doesn't stop *to rain* / *raining* there.

2 Read Jamie's composition. Write *T* for true or *F* for false.

Our clothes project

Last week, my friends and I started a project for school. While we were talking about fashion, we started to think about people who haven't got enough clothes. We decided to send good clean clothes to people in other countries who really need them. We asked our friends and families to bring clothes to the school on Sunday morning.

In the basement of my house, I found lots of great clothes. I enjoyed looking in all our boxes! I found a blue tracksuit that I really liked wearing when I was very young. There was also a pair of new trainers which my sister has never worn and a black raincoat which Mum doesn't need. Dad gave me some good belts and a few T-shirts which he doesn't wear anymore.

On Sunday morning, I took the clothes to the school. All my school friends brought some too. Our teacher is going to send the clothes this week. She was really happy because we wanted to help other people. We shouldn't just think about buying things for ourselves. We should also think about how to help others around us.

1 Jamie had a school project last week. T
2 Jamie and his friends decided to buy some new clothes. ___
3 Jamie found lots of old clothes in his school. ___
4 Jamie's old clothes were in boxes in his house. ___
5 Jamie's sister wore the trainers when she was young. ___
6 Jamie thinks it's a good idea to help others. ___

3 Read again. In which paragraph does Jamie say

1 what they did on Sunday? ___
2 what Jamie and his friends decided to do? ___
3 where he started to collect clothes? ___

Composition (narrative): writing about a project using clothes to help others — Writing 10

4 Complete Jamie's writing plan.

Title: Our clothes project
Paragraph 1: say ¹ _____
Paragraph 2: say ² _____ , say what my family gave
Paragraph 3: say ³ _____ , say how I felt

5 Read another composition. Complete the composition with the sentences from the box.

> It was fun going into the different shops.
> Lots of people came to it and we sold everything.
> ~~We all agreed to ask people to give us things for our bazaar.~~
> My team worked hard and they didn't just think about themselves.
> We got three lovely dresses and nice pink ties with blue stripes.

Our bazaar

Last week, my football team decided to have a bazaar to collect money for people in need.
¹ We all agreed to ask people to give us things for our bazaar.

My friends and I went around the shops in the shopping centre.
² _____ We met lots of people in the shops and told them about the bazaar. They gave us a pair of green boots and lots of pairs of tights at one shop. Then Pat's Designs agreed to give us lots of clothes.
³ _____

On Saturday afternoon, we took everything to the sports centre and got ready for the bazaar.
⁴ _____ Tomorrow we're going to send the money we made to a group which helps children abroad. I'm happy because everyone wanted to help.
⁵ _____

Now it's your turn!

6 Imagine that you have decided to help children in other countries. Use Jamie's writing plan to make notes for your composition below.

My writing plan notes
Title: _____
Paragraph 1: _____
Paragraph 2: _____
Paragraph 3: _____

7 Now use your writing plan to write a composition. Write in your notebook.

Irregular verbs

Infinitive	Past simple	Past participle	Infinitive	Past simple	Past participle
be	was/were	been	lead	led	led
become	became	become	leave	left	left
begin	began	begun	lend	lent	lent
blow	blew	blown	lose	lost	lost
break	broke	broken	make	made	made
bring	brought	brought	meet	met	met
build	built	built	pay	paid	paid
buy	bought	bought	put	put	put
catch	caught	caught	read	read	read
choose	chose	chosen	ride	rode	ridden
come	came	come	ring	rang	rung
cut	cut	cut	run	ran	run
do	did	done	say	said	said
draw	drew	drawn	see	saw	seen
drink	drank	drunk	sell	sold	sold
drive	drove	driven	shine	shone	shone
eat	ate	eaten	sing	sang	sung
fall	fell	fallen	sit	sat	sat
feed	fed	fed	sleep	slept	slept
feel	felt	felt	speak	spoke	spoken
find	found	found	spend	spent	spent
fly	flew	flown	stand	stood	stood
forget	forgot	forgotten	swim	swam	swum
get	got	got	take	took	taken
give	gave	given	teach	taught	taught
go	went	gone	tell	told	told
grow	grew	grown	think	thought	thought
have	had	had	understand	understood	understood
hear	heard	heard	wake	woke	woken
hit	hit	hit	wear	wore	worn
hurt	hurt	hurt	win	won	won
keep	kept	kept	write	wrote	written
know	knew	known			

Notes